See You
on the
Radio

See You on the Radio

on the

Radio

Charles Osgood

G. P. PUTNAM'S SONS
New York

G. P. Putnam's Sons
Publishers Since 1838
a member of
Penguin Putnam Inc.
375 Hudson Street
New York, NY 10014

Library of Congress Cataloging-in-Publication

Osgood, Charles.
See you on the radio / Charles Osgood.
p.   cm
ISBN 0-399-14542-7
PN4874.078A25   1999   99-26958 CIP
814'.54—dc21

Printed in the United States of America

1   3   5   7   9   10   8   6   4   2

This book is printed on acid-free paper.♾

BOOK DESIGN BY AMANDA DEWEY

Acknowledgments

I owe a great deal to many people, and I want you all to know that the check is in the mail. But seriously, folks, this book would not exist as a book were it not for the invaluable assistance of Phil Chin, who produced the "Osgood File's" radio broadcasts it is made up of. There would be no book without Bob Tomlin of CBS, who found the scripts in the computer archives and transferred years of transcribed material so that I could separate the wheat from the chaff. There was a lot more chaff than wheat, believe me. And if Vahé Tchaghlasian hadn't picked out the right computer for me (a Macintosh PowerBook G3), set it up for me and showed me how to use it, there wouldn't be a book, either. I am also grateful for the patience and gentle guidance of Neil Nyren at Putnam. Especially since he'd been through this before with me and knew what he was getting into. And finally a thanks to my many CBS colleagues, past and present, who have inspired me by example and saved my neck a thousand times.

TO MARY ANN MANGUM,

my Irish twin sister who was my very first
audience and who still listens and laughs
better than anyone I know. In radio and
television, even if there are millions of people
tuned in, you have to imagine you are
speaking to only one. The one person
I'm speaking to is Mary Ann.

Contents

Preface

It has been said of radio and television broadcasts that, like cheese or sausage, you will enjoy them more if you never actually see how they are made. This may also be true of books, I have come to believe, and doubly true of one such as this, which contains pieces and essays originally written for broadcast.

Even though I have more standing and experience as a broadcaster than as an author, I must admit that book standards are higher. It is a painful exercise to go over several years of daily effort and confront the awful truth that most of it, for one reason or another, won't measure up. I had imagined that a collection of my best work would be a much thicker book than this one is.

However, what you see before you *does* measure up, I think. Some of the pieces are humorous, some serious, all have to do with the things people are up to. That can be pretty dumbfounding sometimes, and other times positively inspiring.

One thing I should warn you about: most of us broadcast reporters are notoriously poor spellers. We have no experience with it, you see. We tend to sneer when our print media counterparts interrupt someone at a news conference to ask how a name is spelled. We broadcasters never have to do that. Not because we know the spelling, but because we don't care. Being a radio broadcaster in particular means never having to spell anything.

Since the pieces from which this book was created were typed from the audiotapes of actual radio broadcasts, the transcriber spelled all the proper nouns the way they sounded to him or her. Names of people and places are, of course, *not* always pronounced as they sound. Please accept my apology if I've mangled a name in the pages that follow.

Finally, people are always commenting to me about the phrase I use: "See you on the radio." That's impossible, they say, you can't *see* anything on the radio. And now, I fear, calling a book by that title is only going to add fuel to their fire. To them, I have only this to say in defense:

"See you on the radio" . . . I say that every week.
A peculiar phrase, some people think, for anyone to speak.
I've got a piece of mail or two, up on my office shelf,
Complaining that the sentence seems to contradict itself.
"Dear Mr. Osgood," someone wrote. "That sign-off is absurd.

Radio is for the ear . . . the song or spoken word.
The medium for seeing is, without a doubt, TV.
We therefore call it 'video.' That's Latin for 'I see.'
So please don't say that anymore. You really should know better."
That's a gentle paraphrase of what was in this viewer's letter.
"Dear Sir," I then wrote back to him, and this was my reply:
I do believe that you are wrong, and let me tell you why.
I've worked some years in radio, and television, too.
And though it's paradoxical, it nonetheless is true
That radio is visual, much more so than TV.
And there's plenty of good reason why that paradox should be.
You insist that on the radio, there are no pictures there.
You say it's only for the ear . . . but I say, "Au contraire."
There are fascinating pictures on the radio, you see,
That are far more picturesque than any pictures on TV.
No television set that's made, no screen that you can find,
Can compare with that of radio: the theater of the mind.
Where the pictures are so vivid, so spectacular and real,
That there isn't any contest, or at least that's how I feel.
The colors are more colorful, the red and greens and blues.
And more vivid, yet more subtle, than television's hues.
The dimensions of the radio are truly to be treasured:
Infinite the size of screen diagonally measured,
With resolution so acute TV cannot compare.
We can whisper in the listener's ear and take him anywhere.
And you tell me that I cannot see the audience I touch?
Let me tell you now a secret . . . my experience is such
That although the room I work in may be very plain and small . . .
In a way that's quite miraculous, it isn't small at all.

I am there inside the radio, the one beside the bed.
And it's me you hear when it goes off . . . come on now, sleepy-
*   head.*
I can see you in the morning. . . I can see you coast to coast
As you sip your glass of orange juice and bite into your toast.
I am with you as you brush your teeth and as you shave your
*   face.*
You may think you are alone, but I am with you everyplace.
As car radios tune in each morning to "The Osgood Files,"
I see the lines of traffic stretching endlessly for miles.
Not a hundred or a thousand miles . . . a million there must be.
And I'm riding along with them. This is radio, you see.
And I'm on the Jersey Turnpike, on the Thruway and the Hutch,
And the Eisenhower Expressway, helping people keep in touch,
And the California freeways and the Houston traffic funnel.
I may lose you for a little while as you go through the tunnel.
But suddenly I'm there again, some episode to tell,
To nobody's surprise, because they know me very well.
For my voice is with them every day and when it disappears,
They know it comes right back again, it's been that way for years.
I've been riding with them every day for such a long, long time
They are willing to put up with me when I resort to rhyme.
And that may be the ultimate and quintessential test
That proves beyond the slightest doubt that radio is best.
A friend will always stick with you . . . though your poems may
*   not scan.*
I'll see you on the radio . . . I can, you see, I can.

Hazards of Modern Living

I.

Sleepwalking with
the Alligators

There's an old saying that when you're up to your armpits in alligators it's hard to remember sometimes that your original intention was to drain the swamp. Well, now from Palm Harbor, Florida, comes the story of a retiree whose original intention was to get a night's sleep and who found himself up to his armpits in alligators.

James Currans is seventy-seven years old. He's a retired maintenance supervisor living in Palm Harbor, Florida. The other night he must have been sleepwalking, he figures, and somehow tumbled down an embankment into the pond in back of his house. He woke up to find himself in a few feet of mud and water. He was carrying his cane, and tried to use it to lift himself from the muck. But try as he might, he couldn't. And as he thrashed around, he attracted some company. Alligators. Several of them . . . some of them three feet long or bigger.

He poked at them with his cane, and they retreated but kept coming back, and there seemed to be more and more of them. After struggling for about an hour, Currans started yelling. But his wife, Barbara, was sound asleep and couldn't hear him. However, a little girl who lives across the pond heard him. Six-year-old Victoria Martin woke up her mother who called 911. And when firefighters and Pinellas County sheriff's deputies got there at five in the morning, they could hear Currans, too. They couldn't see him because it was still dark. And when they cast a light, all they could see was alligators. Eight or ten of them had Currans surrounded . . . and were only a few feet away from him.

Sheriff's Corporal James Cooper ran, jumped a couple of fences, and spotted Currans up to his waist in water. And while firefighters and other deputies scared the alligators off with their lights, Cooper waded into the mud and rescued Currans. He's okay, except for some cuts on his legs and arms from the fall down the embankment. His wife Barbara tells him: "Jim, you're darn lucky those alligators didn't get ahold of you." This is true. This is *very* true.

The Great
Suburban Oil Spill

Oil tankers are to oil what armored cars are to money. They deliver it from one place to another, unless of course they spill it en route. From time to time, I've taken note of the fact that both conveyances seem to have an unfortunate tendency to leak. There are repeated news stories about both. The rear doors of armored trucks keep springing open, spilling money out all over the road, creating both chaos and delight out there on the highways and byways of America.

But nobody is delighted when the oil tankers run aground, or for some other reason spill oil into the waterways. Surely, we keep saying, there must be some way to keep the money in the trucks and the oil in the tankers. State and federal laws do try to encourage this, but Murphy's Law keeps working against it. Murphy recently visited Cranston, Rhode Island.

That's where John Cienzo lives. The last thing he ever thought would happen is that he would be the victim of an oil spill. For one thing, his house isn't on the water, where an oil tanker spill might foul the beach. For another, the Cienzos don't use oil. They converted to natural gas many years ago. When they converted the boiler, they had the old oil tank cut up and taken out of the basement, so there was no tank that could possibly leak.

John Cienzo's chances of having an oil spill seem remote indeed. The Cienzos never even thought about oil, but they're thinking about it now. This past Saturday, they did have an oil spill. The basement floor was flooded with oil to a depth of three inches. The house had to be evacuated because of the danger posed by the oil fumes.

How could this be? Well, the Cienzos' neighbor across the street still uses oil for heat, and the truck driver who came to deliver oil on Saturday got confused. Maybe Victoria Street looked different in the snow. Anyway, for whatever reason, the oil man made a mistake, went to the wrong house, and hooked his hose up to a spigot that used to lead to the Cienzos' old oil tank and now leads to nothing.

The oil was pumped directly from the tank truck right into the basement, 125 gallons of it. At least there were no fish or birds down there that might be killed, but everything stored there is well lubricated, I can tell you. Officials from the Rhode Island Department of Environmental Management and Clean

Harbors were called to the scene to supervise the cleanup. They say the oil spigot should have been removed at the same time the oil tank was.

It's icy right now in Rhode Island. The Cienzos' driveway might be a little slippery, but not as slippery as their basement.

The Truth Fairy

A large man with the build of a football player got into a van parked outside a grocery store in Rosemont, Minnesota, started up the motor and drove off, just as the couple whose car it was came out of the store.

Well, they called the police. Squad cars set off after the stolen vehicle, a Plymouth Grand Voyager, and caught up with it and pulled it over, and the driver apologized profusely and said something about needing some money for the tooth fairy. Would you believe that, if you were the police officer? Well, this one did believe it, and he was right to do so, because it was true.

The man built like a football player explained that he actually was a football player, a member of the Minnesota Vikings, center Mike Morris, and he produced identification to prove it.

What had happened was that his son, Steven, had lost one of his first teeth, and Morris wanted to play tooth fairy and had gone out to find a silver dollar or two to put under Steven's pillow. And he had driven his mother's Grand Voyager to several stores, trying to find silver dollars, and finally did find a couple, and leaving the place, he got into a Plymouth Grand Voyager, thinking it was his mother's. It looked just like hers, except that it had Iowa plates, which Morris didn't notice.

The key fit the ignition, so he started it up and off he went, and it wasn't until later, when he saw the squad car with flashing red lights coming up behind him, and heard the siren, that he knew anything was wrong.

And it was only when they made him step out of vehicle and showed him the out-of-state license plate that Morris realized that this was not his mother's car after all. Once he was able to establish who he was, and they checked, and sure enough, there was another Grand Voyager much like his mother's parked not far from the other one, they drove him back there, where the owners got their van back and a Mike Morris autograph, and next morning, when little Steven Morris woke up, he found two silver dollars under his pillow.

So you see, there is a tooth fairy, although he may not look exactly as you would picture him.

The Beauty
Contest Fight

I t is good to be competitive. In a world of winners and losers, winning is seen as success and losing as failure. It's thrilling to win and agonizing to lose. The Buffalo Bills, after a winning season, get no credit for what they achieved, only scorn for what they failed to achieve. That is not fair or just, but it seems to be the way people think now. "A good loser," they say, "is a loser." Whatever happened to sportsmanship? If all these violent sports such as pro football, wrestling and figure skating are getting you down, perhaps it's time to turn to a gentle, old-fashioned competition that's really more of a beauty contest than it is a sport. It takes place every year in Chatswater, England. And, in fact, it is a beauty contest. Select the young woman who, by virtue of her beauty, charm and grace, will bear the title of Miss Cornish Tin.

Chatswater is in Cornwall, in the southwest part of England, where they did mine tin once upon a time, although the tin mines there are closed now. The contestants in this event are young beauty queens from villages and towns all over Cornwall.

It was a lovely evening, for the most part. The winner was fourteen-year-old Emma Miller. The first runner-up was Heidi Dark, also fourteen, and the second runner-up was twenty-two-year-old Samantha Lowe. Everything went quite smoothly until the winners were announced, at which point the second runner-up, Ms. Lowe, ran up to the first runner-up, Ms. Dark, and punched her in the face, giving her a black eye, and pushed her and kicked her in the shin and knocked her down to the ground.

The mother of the first runner-up came running up to try to put a stop to this, and she got pushed and whacked on the head—not very ladylike to say the least. The contest winner, wearing the Miss Cornish Tin sash, somehow managed to make herself scarce and escaped involvement in any of this.

Ms. Lowe later explained to the court that it was Heidi Dark's father who had provoked her by walking into the changing room earlier in the evening while she was in her underwear and accusing Ms. Lowe of calling his daughter a slut.

Fiercely competitive, that Miss Cornish Tin contest. Nice change of pace, though, from the figure skating.

The Morning After

Work rules vary from place to place and job to job, but most employers certainly let you take a day off when you're sick, and they don't dock your pay for it. However, Emerson Phillips' boss didn't want to give him sick pay for a day that he took off, because Phillips had announced in advance that this would be the day after his daughter's wedding and he probably would have too much to drink and he would be too sick to come in to work at the Metropolitan Toronto Housing Authority the next day. Therein lies the controversy.

Phillips announced in advance that he believed there was an excellent chance that he wouldn't be working on one certain Monday, since his daughter would be getting married on

See You on the Radio

Sunday. Phillips had good reason, therefore, to think that he just might have one wee bit too much to drink. And so then it wasn't too much of a trick to figure the next day he might call in sick—which he did, just the way he correctly predicted. But the boss said that sickness had been self-inflicted and therefore, for not coming in the next day, he could not expect to collect any sick pay.

Now, is a man sick who is slightly hungover?
It's a question that does come up over and over.
If your tongue is in misery, swollen and dry,
If your head seems to tell you you're going to die,
If you're bleary-eyed, nauseous, and in a bad mood,
And you have a hard time holding down any food,
And you feel like a horse gave you quite a big kick,
Then it would seem to me you are probably sick.

At the Housing Authority, Em Phillips' boss,
Didn't see why the agency should take the loss.
Since this was what Phillips had anticipated,
His boss said the sickness was premeditated.
He said knowing that he would be drinking too much
Disqualified Em from the sick pay as such.
That was the crux of the whole situation,
Which was finally settled by arbitration.

It seemed quite clear to the arbitrator
That if a man drinks he might pay for it later.
The fact that he warned that he might not come in,

Was irrelevant. Emerson Phillips would win.
And ordered to pay him his sick day pay pronto
Was the Housing Authority of Toronto.
For the arbitrator has now decreed
That a hungover man is a sick man indeed.

Bad Stuff in
the Workplace

Nicholas Vierwell of Denver is a good person whose job is to promote safety. What he does at the plant where he works is to load a charge into a small explosive device called an initiator. It inflates car airbags to prevent injury in the event of a collision. One day, however, there was an explosion in the loading machine and the initiator, this tiny little explosive device, got stuck up one of Mr. Vierwell's nostrils and he was afraid if he tried to dig it out, it might go off.

This initiator packs the equivalent of five big M-80 firecrackers, not the kind of thing you want to explode in your nose. It would have killed him if it had gone off, so he didn't want to sneeze or even sniffle with that thing in there. He was escorted to the hospital by the county sheriff's officers and the bomb squad. Then, with the bomb squad and surgical team dressed in lead-lined gowns, Dr. Michael Gordon operated partly under water, since the initiator is activated by air, and very slowly and carefully removed the loaded thing from Mr. Vierwell's nose. Imagine how good it must feel not to have a live explosive device up your nose anymore.

A bad thing happened to Linda Jeffrey, a forty-six-year-old school secretary, of Palmdale, California, when she went to the dentist to have her teeth cleaned. Another Dr. Gordon, Russian-trained dentist Leonid Gordon, told her her teeth were so rotten that they would all fall out in a few months anyway, so she let him pull them all and replace them with dentures. A few years later, something bad happened to Dr. Gordon. In the biggest dental malpractice judgment in California history, Ms. Jeffrey was awarded $1.2 million. She says she's very pleased with the verdict. Now that she's won she's going to look into the possibility of getting dental implants.

Finally, several bad things happened to Frank Curtis when he tried to burglarize the Dog House Deli in Pensacola, Florida. Trying to squeeze his way in through an air vent, he fell through the ceiling and got trapped inside. When he tried to climb out by standing on a sink, the sink collapsed. The pipes broke, water started shooting all over the place, soaking him to the skin. Somewhere along the line, he triggered a silent alarm that called the cops, who say they caught him wet-handed, still carrying the cash from the cash register. Bad night all around for Frank Curtis.

A Slap in the Face

Police officers are human, too. They have feelings and they react to things the same way anybody else would. People sometimes forget that.

In Stillwater, Oklahoma, police Sergeant John Jerkins, a married man with four children, got up at one o'clock in the morning to guide his visiting young nephew to the bathroom. He flipped on a light in the living room, and there were his seventeen-year-old daughter and her boyfriend, also seventeen, having sex on the couch in the living room.

Seeing them there was the last thing he expected. Seeing him there was the last thing they expected, I'll bet. Jerkins yelled at the young man and slapped him across the face, as a lot of fathers might have done under the circumstances. But as a consequence of that slap, he was demoted by the Stillwater Police, lost his sergeant's rank, along with $705 a month in pay and $350 a month in pension benefits. Jerkins has appealed and an arbitrator is weighing that appeal.

Meanwhile, the city of Stillwater, Oklahoma, has upheld Jerkins' demotion and pay cut. A police officer isn't supposed to slap anybody, even if it's a teenage boy he caught having sex with his teenage daughter on the living room couch in the middle of the night in the officer's own house. This does not seem fair to Jerkins. He wants his old rank back and he wants his old pay restored.

He has been on the Stillwater police force for nineteen years and he has a reputation for keeping his cool. But Stillwater city attorney Mary Ann Kearns says if for some reason this officer can no longer maintain the control he is famous for, he is at risk on the street, and it can be a risk for the public.

This was not the street, of course. It happened in his house, in his living room, on his couch, and it was his daughter with whom the teenager he slapped had been having sex.

There has been a great outcry on Jerkins' behalf. Oklahoma's governor, Frank Keating, says he would have hit the boy harder. Jude Metcalf, the son of another Stillwater policeman, says, "They say you're a cop twenty-four hours, but you're a father before that."

District Attorney Robert Hudson says, "We know the climate in Oklahoma. People think that that is conduct you might expect from a parent." Jerkins says, "This isn't just about me. It's about parents and what their duties and responsibilities are and what they can legally do in their own home."

We'll see what happens.

Guns Don't Rob People.
Rocks Rob People.

The National Rifle Association has often made the point that even if guns were outlawed, outlaws would still manage to get guns somehow and would not be deterred by the fact that guns were illegal. The gun lobby argues that if robbers were concerned about violating the law, they wouldn't be robbers in the first place. Also, the NRA reasons, if a holdup man wants to hold somebody up and can't get a gun, he would simply carry out the holdup with some other weapon. I'll admit that this argument seemed a little bit farfetched to me, but maybe the NRA is right. I saw a story on the news wires about a man in Charlotte, North Carolina, who held up a convenience store armed with a rock.

The rock-wielding bandit walked into a QuikShoppe

convenience store early in the morning. The only customer in the store at the time was a woman who worked as a topless dancer at a nearby club. The gunless stickup man grabbed the customer and pointed the rock at the one clerk who was on duty and demanded all the money from the cash register. When he got that, he took all the money the clerk and the customer had on them and then ran off.

So it is demonstrably true, then, that you can hold up a convenience store with a rock, and rocks of all shapes and sizes are freely available in this country. You don't need to get a rock license. You don't have to fill out any forms or divulge any previous criminal record in order to get a rock. You don't have to register a rock. Rocks are cheap and they are so plentiful, in fact, that there are signs here and there across the country warning people to beware of falling rocks. I have never seen a falling gun sign anywhere, have you? Although a flying bullets warning might be appropriate in some places.

Following up on this rock-wielding bandit, however, I can tell you that when he ran out of the QuikShoppe the other day, he was chased by a bunch of teenagers who were apparently not intimidated by the rock. They tackled him, knocked him down, made him spill the money he was carrying, scooped it up, ran off with it and made a clean getaway, leaving the robber and his rock behind in the street. So no need yet for rock control.

HPF

(The Human Perversity Factor)

II

Don't Rush Me!

Does it seem to you that when someone gets into a car to pull out of a parking space, and you're waiting to park in that space and the person in the car sees you and knows that you're waiting to park, that it takes that person forever to start up the car and get out of there? Does it really take people longer to pull out of a parking space if someone's waiting to use that space, or is it just you being paranoid? You'll be pleased to hear that you are not being paranoid. Drivers really do slow down and take their sweet time when they know that someone's waiting. And if you honk the horn, it only makes things worse; they'll slow down even more. And I'm not just making this up. There was a study done by Penn State University. Many tests

confirm how nasty many people are when they get behind a
steering wheel and start to drive a car.

He might be Mr. Nice Guy who takes the world in stride,
But behind the wheel, Mr. Nice Guy turns into Mr. Hyde.
When he sees that you are waiting for the space that he is in,
A slow and lengthy ritual he's likely to begin.
Before he turns the key, he must adjust the rearview,
Find another dozen things that need adjusting, too.
He checks the mileage and the station his radio is set to
And reaches for something apparently quite hard to get to.
He searches through the glove compartment and the space
  beneath,
Then combs his hair and picks at something caught between his
  teeth.

A Penn State study says all this occurs at slower pace
When someone else is clearly waiting for the parking space.
It may not be done on purpose, says the study's editorial,
But rather as expression of an instinct territorial.
This instinct everybody has becomes a little stronger
And causes us to make those waiting wait a little longer.
They checked cars pulling in and out of an Atlanta mall
And clocked how long it took, about four hundred cars in all,
And when someone else was waiting, those who pulled out took
  a notion
To do a dozen things or two and do them in slow motion.

So while you wait and drum your fingers, more and more
  annoyed,

It is not just your impatience, you're not being paranoid.
But when it is your turn to leave, says this report didactic,
The odds are then that you yourself may well employ this tactic.
There's a name unscientific for those who act this way.
I will not tell you what it is, but it starts with an A.

Pleasing
the Pollsters

Do people lie to pollsters? Well, it depends on what you mean by lying. At a big meeting of pollsters and academics in Norfolk recently, they discussed something the polling specialists call self-presentation bias, which is the term for telling a pollster not what you really think, but what you want people to think you think.

Social desirability sounds like something that is socially desirable, wouldn't you say? But it is the bane of people who make a living in the survey business. People have set ideas about what is socially desirable and undesirable, and they don't want anybody to think they aren't doing what they're supposed to be doing, or thinking what they're supposed to be thinking.

Politicians often cite survey results to support some position or another, when, in fact, the findings in the surveys might be the result of too many of the people surveyed trying to give socially desirable answers. A person being polled is not just expressing him- or herself on the thing he or she is being asked about. He or she is also expressing something about him- or herself. You know the joke, "Well, enough about me, let's talk about you. What do you think of me?"

Polling is like that. The respondents, as pollsters call their subjects, are not just expressing their opinion about some issue out there in the world, they're also trying to help the outside world form an opinion about them. We wouldn't want the world to think that we're going around thinking things that the world wouldn't approve of if they thought we were thinking them, would we?

So much for the margin of error! For pollsters, the problem arises when surveys ask about sensitive topics, such as sex, drug use, income, church attendance, how much interest you really had in following the O. J. Simpson trial. A series of surveys over the past eight years by the Pew Research Center for People and the Press found the public expressing little interest in stories about celebrity marriages and scandals, but more often able to answer factual questions about those stories than about more substantive issues of the day.

Ask New Yorkers what paper they read and most will tell you the *Times*. Look around the subway car though and what are they reading? The *Daily News*!

Employee Morale

There are things that everybody knows, and some of them are even true. But you have to watch out for things that everybody knows because some of them are not true. We all know, for example, that happy, cheerful workers make for a happy, cheerful workplace. They're bound to be more productive than someplace where the workers are sad and blue and down in the mouth all the time. But a new study done in Oslo has found exactly the opposite. According to Geir Kaufmann, a professor of psychology at the Norwegian College of Business, a lot of people do their very best work when they are depressed.

It is so much an article of faith with so many people that happy, cheerful workers do better work that many employers have taken to using certain colors, certain lighting or piped-in music to put their employees in a good mood. But if Professor Kaufmann is correct, the boss might be better off if the workers weren't quite so happy. Kaufmann says that cheerful test subjects tend to overestimate their own ability and to underestimate the complexity of the tasks and problems presented to them. And they tend to arrive at solutions that are the easiest and most obvious but not necessarily the best.

The glum people, on the other hand, were less confident and looked deeper and found far more creative solutions to the problems. So heigh-ho, heigh-ho, it's off to work we go, but in the case of the Seven Dwarfs, according to the Kaufmann theory, Grumpy might have put in a more productive workday than Happy. There's a lot of anecdotal evidence of people doing their best work while depressed, says Kaufmann. Einstein once said he was in a sad mood the day he came up with the theory of relativity.

This doesn't mean that employers should run out and buy black paint and recordings of dirges to play on the music system. But it's important that workers not be so entertained on the job that they forget why they're there. Meanwhile, as one of the office signs you can buy puts it: "The beatings will continue until the morale improves."

Politicians and Psychopaths

We hear all too often that people do not like or trust politicians. Not surprising, really, if they believe half the things political candidates say about each other. But perhaps our distrust of politicians is more than just an aversion to negative campaigning. In reporting the results of a three-year study at Caledonian University in Glasgow, Scotland, psychologist David Cooke says that he and his colleagues found that politicians and criminal psychopaths share some important behavioral characteristics, no offense intended.

Far be it from me to suggest that your candidate is a psychopathic liar. I'm sure he or she is a perfectly lovely person who speaks only the truth. But do you trust his or her opponent? See, that's what I thought.

There was once a politician who said, "I am not a crook."
But an eminent psychologist whose name is David Cooke,
Says that there are certain patterns of behavior at times,
Shared by people who do politics and people who do crimes.
"Both appear to be quite prone to certain forms of impropriety,"
Cooke reported to the British Psychological Society.
Psychopaths tend to be grandiose. They do not feel remorse,
And that is often true of politicians, too, of course.
Psychopaths and politicians and stockbrokers, too, says Cooke,
Often have a lot in common when you take a closer look.
Politicians often had a childhood in some way disturbed,
As did many of the psychopaths, Cooke's research team observed.
Troubled childhood seems to be, in fact, a rather common thread,
David Cooke and his research assistant, Lisa Marshall, said.
Psychopaths lie easily and won't say what's really meant.
Politicians do that also, with no criminal intent,
But they do it for a reason, when departing from the truth,
And that is to sway the voters when they're in the voting booth.
It may not hurt a politician, facing what they face;
It may even help a bit to be a psychopathic case.
So you have to listen closely to what politicians tell you
And before you buy the stock that some stockbroker wants to sell
    you.
Not all brokers or politicos are psychopaths, of course.
Not all crooks go into politics; that's true with equal force.
But the politicians, criminals and brokers that you see,
Have a lot in common with each other and with you and me.

Communicating
Through the Press

Paula Poppy, the evening and weekend receptionist at the Dale Wood Walk-in Clinic in Woodbridge, Virginia, was glancing through the want ads in the local paper, the *Potomac News*. She does that sometimes just for the heck of it, to see what opportunities might be out there. You know what they say, the best time to get a job is when you've already got one.

And one particular ad caught her eye. It was for a receptionist. She looked to see if they mentioned the shift. Maybe she thought she could handle both jobs, I don't know. But they did mention the shift, and it happened to be exactly the same as hers, evenings and weekends. So she looked to see what outfit this was that wanted a new receptionist for the evenings and weekends, and it was the Dale Wood Walk-in Clinic. This was her job that was being offered in the newspaper. What a way to find out they want to get rid of you.

She asked somebody at work if they were looking for somebody to replace her, and she was told, "Well, yes, now that you ask, that is true." So Paula Poppy put on her coat and went over to the newspaper office and wrote out a check for $61.80 to the *Potomac News,* and she took out the following one-inch ad in the classifieds.

"As of this date, I quit," she wrote. "If I had to find out through the newspaper," says Paula, "I decided they could find out through the newspaper, too." The owner of the clinic, Jatenda Wallia, says, "I just don't understand. Doesn't she have the courtesy to tell me she's quitting?" She told them, Paula says. She told them in the newspaper in writing.

Communication, harsh or sweet,
Has to be a two-way street.
Sometimes you talk for what you earn
Sometimes you listen and you learn.
In Paula's case they would replace her
Before they had to go and face her.
She did communicate with candor.
What's good for goose is good for gander.

The Human
Perversity Factor

Anybody who has a dog is probably familiar with what I call the DPF, or Dog Perversity Factor. When my dogs are inside, they always want to go out. When they're outside, they decide pretty soon that they want to come back in.

We humans can certainly relate to that. The grass is always greener for us on the other side of the fence. The HPF, or Human Perversity Factor, is nowhere more in evidence than when our finger is on the thermostat.

It is colder in the winter than it is in the summer. I realize this is not exactly an original observation. You have probably noticed it yourself. But with the HPF, or Human Perversity Factor, there is evidence that we want to feel warmer in the winter than we do in the summer and colder in the summer than we do in the winter.

We consume huge amounts of gas and oil in the wintertime trying to bring the indoor temperature up to levels which, in the summertime, we would regard as too hot. When the summer comes, we consume prodigious amounts of electricity on air-conditioning trying to cool down the indoor temperatures to levels which, in the season when the wind is blowing and the snow is snowing, we would regard as too cold.

In other words, we want the indoors to be the exact opposite of whatever it is outdoors. We can't control the outdoor temperature, but we can and do control the indoor temperatures to a ridiculous extent.

I have friends who, when it is so hot outside you could fry an egg on the sidewalk, keep their apartment so well air-conditioned you could store meat in there. But when it's so cold that winter festivals and ice-fishing tournaments are being canceled left and right because of the deep freeze, they turn the thermostat to the point where you could melt marshmallows over the living room radiator. When the windchill is −25 outside, they like it to be 80 degrees inside. When it's pushing 100 outside, they want it 65 inside. That is a 15-degree HPF differential. We're bad.

The Brain
in Spain

We like to think that we—at least we here in the Western world—are so sophisticated and aware that we can always tell the difference between what's real and what's phony on television. We would never mix up fact with fiction, news with docudrama. We know when it's information we're getting, or entertainment, or somebody's simply selling us something. You would never today be able to fool people and frighten them the way Orson Welles did years ago with his famous Halloween radio broadcast, "The War of the Worlds." Maybe in some primitive Third World backwater you can get people going, ah, but not us Westerners. We're much too smart for that nowadays. Modern Spain is a forward-looking, progressive country. The Spanish people are romantic, it's true, but the land of Cervantes and Picasso is full of sophisticated, well-educated people. They've got TV. They watch CNN. They weren't born yesterday. So it came as something of a surprise when hundreds of panicked Spaniards flooded TV and radio switchboards with calls asking about the space aliens hovering over New York.

What they had seen on the Telecinco network were, in fact, commercials for the American movie *Independence Day*, which was about to open in Spain. The advertising agency, Publi-Espana, figured that viewers would not be fooled by a spoof of "The War of the Worlds."

"We wanted to do something different, cause some excitement, but certainly not fear," said agency executive Jose Luis Andarias. But when the same box gives you both fact and fiction, the lines get blurred sometimes. And when people from Madrid to Barcelona, from Seville to Valencia, saw scenes of a White House press conference about the invasion, and an announcer breaking away to shots of New Yorkers fleeing the streets, they didn't find it any stranger than the real news these days. A text warning on the bottom of the screen said, "Advertisement." "But," says ad man Andarias, "apparently people can't watch footage, listen and read at the same time."

And it's not just the Spanish who have that problem. We all do. Have you ever tried to read that small print that fills the screen in certain commercials, the legal mumbo jumbo that defies all understanding? "Anything heretofore to the contrary notwithstanding."

Too many inputs overload, short-circuiting the brain,
And that's a problem everywhere. It isn't just in Spain.

The Lightning Strike
Victims Convention

At any given time in this country, there are hundreds of con-
ventions going on. Soda jerks convene, Trekkies convene,
doctors and lawyers convene. And in Gettysburg, Pennsylvania,
I found out about a convention of people who have been hit
by lightning. I swear.

Comparing notes, many of those people at the Lightning
Strike Victims Convention have been telling each other they
haven't been the same since it happened. Most of them look
perfectly all right. Tests seem to show they're all right. Doctors
who have examined them say they are all right.

"That's easy for them to say!" says Harold Deal of Green-
wood, South Carolina. He's heard doctors telling him that for
twenty-six years, but he says he knows better. He says he knows

darn well that he has not been the same since a bolt of lightning knocked him clear out of his boots and sent him flying fifty feet back in 1969. Deal says he hasn't been cold since then. He's been hot. It gets hot there in South Carolina in the summertime. Deal claims he likes to fill a bathtub with cold water and put eight bags of ice in there and then get into the tub and sit in the ice water. He has a collage of photographs showing himself romping through snow in nothing but a pair of shorts, each picture labeled with a temperature: 5 degrees, −10 degrees, −44 degrees.

Another conventioneer, Wilhelm Jonacht, says he used to speak eleven languages when he was head chef at the Metropolitan Museum of Art in New York City. Not only that, but he says he was a kung fu grand master who used to run ten miles a day and do three hundred push-ups a day. Now he can only stammer through the simplest conversation. He says he touched something electrical back in 1992 and took 3,900 volts.

There's a doctor who specializes in treating for shocks and lightning strikes. Dr. Hooshang Hooshmand says with lightning and electric shock victims, the body's hardware is usually not damaged, but the software is often scrambled. It should be pointed out that Dr. Hooshmand is only allowed to practice under supervision ever since his conviction on charges of Medicare fraud. Another doctor, Robert Daroff, of the University Hospitals of Cleveland, says many of these people are like other fringe groups. They are people without organic diseases, he says, who are depressed, angry and litigious. Especially when they come into contact with a lawyer.

The Game
of Golf Ball

Ben Seymour of Chattanooga, Tennessee, is seventy years old and a great golf ball enthusiast. Note I didn't say "golf enthusiast"; I said "golf ball enthusiast." He may not be the greatest golfer in the world, but he certainly does have a lot of balls.

BEN SEYMOUR: I have a collection of 6,430 golf balls, all with the logos on them, and there's no two alike.

The only thing Ben Seymour ever did with golf balls was to play golf until one day eleven years ago when Arnold Palmer came to his Tennessee town.

SEYMOUR: He has a business here, and he brought each employee a dozen golf balls, all with different logos on them.

And one sweet lady that worked there didn't play golf, so she gave me her dozen. And I looked at them, and I thought, "Oh, these are just too pretty to hit." And that's where my troubles began.

Ben mounted the balls on the walls of his den, and they looked so pretty he thought that he would get a few more. And pretty soon, the room was filled with thousands of golf balls, each with a different insignia or picture.

SEYMOUR: Well, I've got many, many from colleges. And I've got many, many businesses. I've got some with just little sayings on them. I've got one golf ball with the Lord's Prayer on it. Don't ask me why. I guess that golfer thought he would have a better prayer of a chance.

Ben finds balls, buys balls and gets lots of them from friends.

SEYMOUR: I have one golf ball that has an eye on it. And it may be homemade, but it's a good job. And I could imagine some guy beginning to play golf, and someone saying, "Fella, you've got to keep your eye on the ball." So he painted his eye on the ball and still lost it.

Ben's favorite has the words "First golf ball on the moon" printed on one side.

SEYMOUR: One of my buddies said, "Well, Ben, if that golf ball was on the moon, how did you get it?" And I said, "Well, the only way I can figure, the crescent turned up a little too far one night, and it rolled out and fell in my backyard."

Ben has no idea what his collection may be worth, but how sweet it is just to look at them all.

SEYMOUR: Yes, I do have a sweet spot for golf balls in my den.

Boring

One of the worst things you can say about a political candidate is that he or she is boring. It's difficult to generate a lot of excitement and enthusiasm for a candidate who is boring. But in some places there's no getting away from it. In Boring, Oregon, for example, they have a Boring mayor, a Boring council; you could say the same thing about the whole Boring government. They have a Boring Police Department, even a Boring Fire Department. They have a Boring School System, a Boring Library. Sounds as if a terrible case of ennui has settled over the whole town. But, in fact, the people in Boring are not a bit boring. Well, some of them are, I suppose, but most Boringers are anything but, I'm told.

I figure Boring, Oregon, was named after somebody named

Boring. There was a Jeremiah Boring back there somewhere. And he can't have been too boring or they wouldn't have named the whole town after him. Today, since nobody wants to be thought of as boring, my guess is that a lot of people whose names were Boring have had the name changed. I find only one Boring listed in the Manhattan residential phone book, an A. Boring, and one in the business listings, a Z. Boring. That's all the Borings from A to Z.

I'm sure there must be more than that. I've attended hundreds of boring meetings in Manhattan and dozens of boring cocktail parties.

In the Yellow Pages under Boring, I find "Boring Contractors" and "Boring Equipment." In London, if you look up the word "Boring" in the Yellow Pages, it says, "See civil engineers." Civil engineers don't like this one bit. For years now, the Institution of Civil Engineers has lobbied for a new directory listing. Their friends would make jokes about it. The same joke, actually: "Looked in the phone book today, Nigel. Found you listed under 'Boring.'"

The trade publication *Tunnels and Tunneling* is widely known as "Bores and Boring." Editor Mike Page, who is responsible for all the advertising pages in the magazine as well, says, "All tunnels involve boring, but the people in the industry are not boring, I assure you."

The Yellow Pages publishers have agreed to change the listing, so that under Boring it says, "See site exploration."

Slackers

The Random House *Webster's College Dictionary* people are out with another revised edition, containing some six hundred words that weren't included in the last edition. One of the new words is sheesh—S-H-E-E-S-H—an interjection, the new revision says, used to express exasperation. I mention sheesh first because some of the other new words and definitions seem to me to be eminently sheeshable, if you accept that definition of sheesh, which I'm not sure I do.

There are more words in the language than there are in the dictionary. That is always true, and that is why it's necessary from time to time to publish revised editions to incorporate some of the gazillion words out there—or should I say the word gazillion that's now in there. Gazillion, defined as an extremely large, indeterminate number.

Of course, there are other words that you could define in exactly the same way. What is a jillion, if not that? And for that matter, what is a zillion? And what's the difference between a zillion and a gazillion? Is a jillion larger or smaller than a zillion or a gazillion?

"Indeterminate" sure covers a multitude of meanings, doesn't it? I mean, sheesh, let's get more precise here—as in, a zillion is a jillion to the umpteenth power or something like that.

According to this new dictionary, netiquette and rocumentary are both words. Netiquette being etiquette on a computer network, especially the Internet, and a rocumentary being a documentary about rock musicians.

And here is one that I have to say I totally disagree with. Slacker is in there as a noun, defined as an educated young person who is anti-materialistic, purposeless, apathetic and who usually works in a dead-end job. Well, excuse me—or maybe I should say, well, sheesh. In my humble, non-lexicographic opinion, that fails to meet all the tests of a definition. Can you be a slacker without being well educated? Yes. Can you be anti-materialistic without being a slacker? Of course you can. Are there slackers who do not have dead-end jobs or people who have dead-end jobs who aren't slackers? You bet.

A lexicographer I'm not, nor could I ever be one,
But even I can recognize a slacker when I see one.

The Dave Factor

As a Dave Barry fan, I was fascinated recently to hear that the Daves of the world are uniting. Dave Moore of Greeley, Colorado, says the more Daves there are in this world, the better.

DAVE MOORE: They're easygoing. They have good senses of humor. They're, of course, very brave and intelligent.

Dave recently opened up the Dave Hall of Fame in—wouldn't you know it?—David City, Nebraska. Not too much to it. At the moment it's little more than a post office box number, 54.

MOORE: We just have newspaper articles and photographs at this time. We're hoping that as word gets out, we'll have more memorabilia of things Dave to include in it. And also we hope to expand it into a larger structure, perhaps P.O. Box 175.

The Hall of Fame inductees include some big-name Daves.

MOORE: We have Dave Letterman, who was also named Dave of the Year. We have Dave Winfield, who got his three thousandth hit.

OSGOOD: By the way, Dave, who's your favorite Dave?

MOORE: King David, because if it weren't for King David, many of us would be named Goliath.

Dave Moore also heads Daves International, a club open to anyone named Dave or David, although female Davidas or surnamed Davidsons are welcome too. Besides giving Daves the respect they deserve, the group also engages in an outreach program.

MOORE: We've heard from Consolidated Larrys, based in Lawrence, Kansas, and then we're also trying to get together with Global Georges.

Daves International also welcomes new converts.

MOORE: We believe that there will be a lot of Dave wannabes out there, and we are going to set up a program whereby people can have their names legally changed to Dave.

Dave Moore is more or less willing to name honorary Daves, although it's clear his standards for that are not too high.

MOORE: Well, yeah, Charlie, we'd be happy to make you an honorary Dave. Consider yourself a Dave. I think "Dave Osgood" has a good ring.

III.

Law
and
Order

Lawyers' Rice Bowl

You can write a book about the law without being a lawyer. Hey, it's a free country. Anybody can write a book about anything, right? Well, not so fast. If you write a book about how a person can act as his own lawyer—even if you *are* a lawyer—you *know* who isn't going to like it, don't you? Other lawyers, of course! They charge fancy money for the sort of advice that's in the *Be Your Own Lawyer* books. In Texas right now some attorneys are charging a California publisher— Nolo Press—with practicing law without a license.

The San Francisco publishing firm was founded by a couple of lawyers with the idea of helping the public deal with the legal system without going to the expense of hiring a lawyer. They've got 150 different manuals on everything from divorce to wills to copyrights. Lawyers charge by the hour for their services. Two hundred dollars an hour is not unusual. Some charge more. The Nolo manuals sell for less than fifty bucks. But some lawyers in Texas are now saying that what Nolo is doing is practicing law without a license. That's illegal in all states. Texas is the only state so far to apply that to book publishing. The Texas State Bar's Unauthorized Practice of Law Committee has argued in the past that books advising the public about solving legal problems are as dangerous as bad lawyers.

A statement from Nolo says: "It frightens us that the lawyers in a state can decide that the people in a state aren't going to get the information they need to do their own law." The Texas Bar Committee is investigating several other publishers, too, including the maker of *Quicken Family Lawyer,* which provides instructions for eighty-eight different legal forms. In 1992, the Texas courts upheld a ban on a non-lawyers publication called *You and Your Will: A Do-It-Yourself Manual.* The court said at that time, "The State bar has not only the right but also the obligation to prevent legal advice clothed in the robes of simplicity from adversely affecting the estates of the unsuspecting public."

Well, my guess is that it's the suspecting public buying these books. These are the people who suspect that if they go to a lawyer, whether the advice is any good or not, they'll have to pay an arm and a leg for it.

Mountains Out
of Molehills

It used to be that most little, relatively unimportant infractions of the rules or breaches of decorum wouldn't come to the attention of the authorities. No need to make a federal case out of every little offense. People would just work it out for themselves or let it go. But nobody seems to let anything go anymore.

On October 2, a date that will live in infamy, somebody launched a sneak attack with a paper clip on Suzanne Mensh, the sixty-seven-year-old clerk of the Baltimore County Circuit Court. She was standing in the courthouse, minding her own business, when she felt a sharp pain behind her left ear. And a half-hour later, she walked into the sheriff's office with a ridged paper clip. Somebody—she doesn't know who—had, by some unknown means—a rubber band, perhaps—launched that sneak attack, hitting her in the back of the head. It didn't pierce the skin, cause it to bleed or anything. She didn't need any medical attention. But this, she said, was an unacceptable act, worse than spitting in someone's face.

Spitting in someone's face has become the standard for unacceptable acts in the Baltimore area, as baseball fans may know. Anyway, nobody lets anything slide anymore. Sheriff's deputies are now on the case. They've interrogated witnesses, taken notes, drawn diagrams of the crime scene. This is an assault case now. One of these days, they hope to solve the case of the flying paper clip.

And near Gettysburg, Pennsylvania, thirteen-year-old Christopher Bolinger put a piece of an Alka-Seltzer tablet in his mouth so that it would foam up and it would scare his classmates, or make them laugh at least. Such reasons often seem good enough to thirteen-year-old boys. Ah, but no—no, no, no, nobody lets anything like that go anymore. School officials have been all but foaming at the mouth. Christopher has been suspended from Fairfield Middle School for ten days at least. The officials searched his locker; they notified the police; they referred him to a county drug agency. "I was just acting stupid and goofing around," says the eighth-grader. But the drug policy of the school bans any type of medication. "And besides," says one school district official, "we can't have kids putting things in their mouth that they might not even know what it is. You can overdose on anything."

Well, you can also overreact to anything, too, it seems to me.

The Right
to Snore

As you know, the United States Supreme Court only hears cases involving important constitutional questions.

It has never in its long and august history had occasion to consider a snoring case. But there is one in Davis, California, right now, the landmark case of *Dougherty* v. *Saed,* which involves questions as basic as life, liberty and the pursuit of a good night's sleep. It seems to have Supreme Court written all over it.

There is nothing in the U.S. Constitution specifically about the right to a good night's sleep. However, it could be argued that to be deprived of a good night's sleep in effect rules out much life, liberty and happiness or the pursuit thereof.

A Davis woman, Sari Saed, apparently snores so loudly that

her next-door neighbor, Chris Dougherty, says he cannot sleep. It happens their bedrooms are on either side of a common wall. So Mrs. Saed, a mother of two, was hauled into court the other day for violating the Davis noise ordinance.

If convicted, she faces a $50 fine. But she pleaded not guilty, has hired a lawyer of her own, because she's the one who can't get a night's sleep anymore because every time she does, she snores. And every time she snores, Dougherty bangs on the wall and wakes her up. And he's the one who's not letting her get any sleep. One night he even went so far as to call the cops. Apparently, she wakes him up by snoring, and then he wakes her up to get her to stop snoring, and she's afraid to go back to sleep for fear that she'll start snoring again.

The Davis City Council ruled that snoring is not willful volition. She wasn't snoring on purpose, or anything like that. And the law specifically prohibits people from willfully making any noise which causes discomfort or annoyance to any reasonable person of normal sensitivity.

But a citation has been issued, and the city council cannot simply dismiss it. The district attorney's office has to decide now whether to prosecute. Thus begins what could be a historic legal journey up the judicial ladder. You think capital punishment and abortion are difficult legal questions, just wait till the Supreme Court has to deal with its first snoring-rights case.

Too Much
Enthusiasm

Places that serve coffee have had more than their share of lawsuits over the last several years. The most celebrated cases have had to do with hot coffee being too hot and the plaintiffs suing for lots of money because they spilled the hot coffee on themselves.

Some places started serving their coffee a little more tepid so as not to tempt more lawsuits. Tepid coffee isn't as good as nice, hot coffee, but you won't get very far trying to sue somebody for a lot of money because their coffee was too tepid.

Anyway, Starbucks is now being sued for an incident that occurred a year ago in Littleton, Colorado, and that has nothing to do with how hot or how strong the Starbucks coffee was.

It has to do with the strength not of the coffee, but of one of the Starbucks employees.

When carpenter and general contractor Jerry Merich went into the Starbucks place in Littleton, Colorado, last summer, one of the employees, Eric Shoemaker, greeted him with a couple of high fives. You know what a high five is. It's a handshake that involves reaching way up in the air with your hand, sometimes with both hands, and slapping the other person's hand or hands. Well, Shoemaker's first high-five swipe there at Starbucks was okay, Merich says, but his second one was so strong that it injured Merich's shoulder, so much so that according to the lawsuit Merich has filed, he was "unable to get work as a carpenter for seven months."

He is seeking damages against the Starbucks chain for that high five for loss of wages and business profits, for pain and suffering, for personal injury and for damage to his business. The shoulder injury has never completely healed, he says, and still requires repeated medical attention. And the exact amount of money isn't specified, but they must figure Starbucks has deep pockets. "Let's go after Starbucks rather than Eric Shoemaker, who, even if we win the case, we wouldn't be able to get a lot of money off because he doesn't have a lot of money." So Shoemaker is not the defendant; Starbucks is.

You know, if anything, it has always seemed to me that high-fiving is a safer way to greet somebody than the old-fashioned, conventional handshake, where some jerk who thinks he's being macho too often gives you the old finger-crusher. It makes you want to spill hot coffee on him.

The Sleeping
Pedestrian

Everywhere you go, it seems there are different traffic laws. Right turns on red lights are not permitted in New York City, for example. Visitors from L.A. are at risk in New York City because they assume pedestrians always have the right of way and New York motorists think that pedestrians are on their own.

Well, even the definition of a pedestrian is not the same everywhere. For the purposes of Colorado's insurance laws, anybody involved in a motor vehicle accident who is not in a motor vehicle is a pedestrian.

Pedestrian comes from *pes, pedis,* the Latin word meaning "foot," and you might think the only way a sleeping person could be a pedestrian would be if he was sleepwalking. How can you be on foot if you are flat on your back? In Colorado it is possible.

In October 1977, Darvin and Jackie Smith and their kids were at home in bed in the middle of the night, sound asleep, when a car, driven by a woman on her way home from a party, went out of control, headed right for the Smiths' house, climbed up the sidewalk, through the outside wall and into the house, crashing into the bedroom of one of the Smith kids.

A crashing, banging, crumbling noise woke Jackie and Darvin up. They rushed into the kids' rooms and found this automobile sitting in the middle of Andrew's room. Both his bedroom and brother Bruce's looked as if they had been bombed. Rubble everywhere. Fortunately, nobody was hurt, but there was an awful lot of damage to the house.

The lawyer for the motorist who drove into the house argued that the Smiths could only claim limited damage because they were pedestrians, and pedestrians are limited as to what they can collect under the no-fault law that was enforced. They were not motorists, were they? They were not passengers, were they? Well, therefore, by process of elimination, they must have been pedestrians.

The Smiths took it to court. And after years of appeals, the judge awarded over $13,000 in compensatory damages and $32,000 in punitive damages. Said the appeals judge, "To include persons secure in their homes and asleep in their beds as pedestrians does not comport with common sense."

Comporting with common sense is rarely required in the law, but it's a refreshing novelty every so often.

When I Was
One and Sixty

Age is a relative thing. It all depends on your perspective. I
can remember thinking that anybody who is the age that
I am now is pretty darn old, one foot in the grave, as they used
to say. Now I can't believe I was ever so young as to have
thought such a silly thing. Age discrimination is illegal now in
this country. You can't just fire somebody who is old and
replace him with somebody who's a lot younger, even if the
younger person is also old. That is what the Supreme Court
now says.

Under the federal Age Discrimination and Employment Law,
your boss can't fire you just because you're over forty years old
and replace you with some young whippersnapper who is
under forty. But the boss who fired James O'Connor from his

manager's job at Consolidated Coin Caterers at the age of fifty-six thought he was on safe ground, because he replaced O'Connor with somebody else who was not under forty. He was forty years old exactly. But O'Connor, who had been running one of the North Carolina company's sales regions, filed an age bias suit anyway, charging that the boss had been making disparaging remarks, telling him he was "too damn old for this kind of work" and that sort of thing.

A lower court had thrown out the case on the grounds that if a forty-year-old replacement was hired, then it couldn't have been age discrimination. But the United States Supreme Court ruled in O'Connor's favor, reinstating his case and sending it back to the lower courts.

"The fact that one person in the protected class has lost out to another person in the protected class is irrelevant," wrote Justice Antonin Scalia, "as long as he has lost out because of his age." So score one for the old folks.

To paraphrase A. E. Housman's poem "A Shropshire Lad":

When I was one and sixty, I heard somebody say,
The boss might look for someone else, and take my job away.
But I found this ridiculous, I thought of it no more,
And did still more of what I did than I had done before.

When I was two and sixty, I told myself again,
That jobs like mine were right for me, but not for younger men.
For I believe experience goes into what I do.
And now I'm three and sixty, and ah 'tis true, 'tis true.

A Word of
Warning

In 1988, a Detroit couple, John and Tina Bennis, bought a 1977 Pontiac for $600. A few months later, John Bennis used that car in picking up a prostitute. Tina didn't know he was going to do this. Husbands don't usually tell their wives, "Well, honey, I'm taking the car for a little while. I'm going to go out and try to pick up a prostitute." And since she didn't know, Mrs. Bennis didn't think it was fair that when her husband was arrested for soliciting a prostitute, the car was seized. There is a law in Michigan that says the government can forfeit property used as a public nuisance. But Tina Bennis hadn't done anything wrong and the car was half hers. She thought, at the very least, if the authorities were going to take the car, they should have paid her for her half. The case went all the way up to the United States Supreme Court.

In a split five-to-four decision, the United States Supreme Court ruled that the state of Michigan was within its rights to seize John and Tina Bennis' car, even if Tina didn't know, as she insists she didn't, that her husband was off trying to pick up a prostitute the night he was arrested and the car was seized, and the state doesn't have to compensate her for her half interest in the car and does not have to prove that she did know about it.

Chief Justice Rehnquist, for the majority, wrote that "an owner's interest in property may be forfeited by reason of the use to which the property is put, even though the owner did not know that it was to be put to that use." Four of the justices dissented, including Justice Stevens, who cited a previous ruling in another case that made forfeiture subject to the Eighth Amendment, which bars excessive fines. "Fundamental fairness prohibits the punishment of innocent people," he wrote.

Banks were interested in this case, because if the authorities can seize cars or boats or whatever without recourse, they can lose their collateral for loans. In this case, the amount of money was only half of $600, but the principle would apply just as much to a $60,000 car as to a $600 car. Legally, if Mrs. Bennis wants to be compensated, she can't go after the state; she'll have to go after her husband, who presumably already had a lot of explaining to do.

So if your spouse or son or daughter or anybody uses the family car, just be aware of what can happen.

The Canine
Kleptomaniac

In Green Oak Township, Michigan, lives a golden retriever who retrieves much more than his master would like him to. Some dogs are smart and learn very quickly. When Dennis and Cindy Grimes wanted to train their retriever, Molson, to go fetch the Sunday morning paper for them, all they had to do was provide him with a little positive reinforcement. When Molson got the paper for them, he would get a bone.

Well, soon Molson began to understand that there was a connection between the bringing of the Sunday paper and the getting of a bone. So not only would he bring them their Sunday newspaper, but also the newspaper of their next-door neighbor and the newspaper of the people who live across the street. It got so Molson would bring them four newspapers every

Sunday. And he would bring home some other things, too, much to the Grimes' embarrassment. He would bring them shoes and boots and lunch bags and all sorts of stuff.

Dennis and Cindy tried to discourage Molson from this sort of behavior. "Bad dog!" they would say. But by now the retriever was retrieving things out of instinct, possibly, and possibly with the forlorn hope that one of these times he would bring them something that they would like as much as they did that Sunday paper that earned him the bone that time.

Well, the Grimes began to rue the day they had ever given the dog a bone and started all this. Over the next several weeks, Molson presented them with a tool box and a hockey puck and many, many other things. The Grimes didn't know which articles came from which neighbors, and so they finally have put a clothes tree up in front of their house to display all the stolen goods so that the neighbors can come by and claim their missing property.

Nowadays if anybody in that part of Livingston County is missing anything, Molson has become the number-one usual suspect. As for the dog himself, he is being kept inside these Sunday mornings, at least long enough to let the local folks retrieve their Sunday papers before the retriever does. They like Molson. He's a nice, friendly animal. But they're keeping their garage doors closed now to discourage his little treasure hunts.

Molson's a splendid retriever, as fine as there ever was.
And I can't help believing he'll keep on retrieving.
That's what a retriever does.

Fugitive
Welfare Rights

Did you know that if you're lying low because you happen to be a convict who jumped bail before sentencing, or if you're wanted for violation of parole or probation, that that doesn't stop you from collecting welfare? Under the law, as currently interpreted, a fugitive's welfare benefits cannot be denied, and the government can't do anything about it. Furthermore, the welfare officials can't turn you in. Privacy laws limit the exchange of information between police and welfare agencies. The agencies have no idea which of their clients are on the lam.

But in Cleveland, where 330 fugitives from justice were rounded up in a six-month sting operation, it turned out that at least ninety-one of them had been on welfare while hiding out. In other words, as one Cleveland law-enforcement officer puts it, "The Department of Human Services had known where these people were living and were subsidizing their criminal activity at taxpayer expense."

If you are a fugitive, if you are on the lam,
The government will pay you. It's a lovely little scam.
While the law is looking for you, while they're searching high
*   and low,*
You can still apply for welfare because nobody will know.
You can give them your full name and current address—what
*   the heck.*
The only way they'd use it is to send you out a check.
And police won't check the welfare rolls to see if you are there.
That would violate your privacy, and so they wouldn't dare.

No matter if you violate probation or parole,
You can hide from the authorities and still be on the dole.
It may not be an awful lot of money that you win,
But it's nice to know you've got a little something coming in.
And if it's not enough and leaves you still a little poor,
You can always find some way to supplement it, I am sure.

The taxpayer behind the check you got today just might,
Be the self-same person you go out and rob tonight.
The fugitive today can hook his thumbs into each ear,
While wiggling his fingers at us, so it would appear.
A fugitive can double-thumb his nose at everyone,
Knowing that the system means that nothing can be done.

Happy Day

In the poor farming community of Indiantown, Florida, some 680 black farm workers showed up yesterday in a sweltering Baptist church, this time not to pray, but to get what they had been praying for, for a good, long time.

They all worked, or used to, for a Martin County citrus grower, Caulkins Indiantown Citrus Company. Twelve years ago, a foreman named John Henry Robinson sued the company, saying black employees weren't being fairly treated, weren't being paid as much as white workers, were consistently subjected to safety hazards and harassment.

The litigation went on and on. It lasted for more than a decade, during which time the company changed ownership. Seven law firms worked on the case, and their legal fees amounted to $5.4 million. By the time the trial was finished last year, there were fifty boxes of paperwork. But in the end, a federal jury sided with the workers, and a settlement was hammered out for thirteen and a half million. The farm workers never thought they'd live to see the day. But yesterday, that day came.

Wilbur Johnson worked for Caulkins Indiantown Citrus Company for nine years as a heavy-equipment operator. They paid him $5.95 an hour to train white workers who started at more than $7 an hour. Yesterday at the church, he was handed a check for $22,000. He says he's going to buy a trailer now. The average check was for about $15,000, but some were for more—for quite a bit more. Charlie Jackson, Jr., who is fifty years old and used to work for Caulkins as a fruit picker and a driver, stared at his check for a long time, made out to him in the amount of $101,096. "You know how good this feels," Charlie Jackson said, "how good we all feel?" He's going to buy a home now. He's never owned a home before. Annie Thornton is going to pay off her mortgage. James Coward's going to fix up his truck.

Henry Robinson, the original plaintiff, the foreman who first brought the complaint to court, will collect close to $750,000! Oh, happy day! Although they didn't gather to pray there yesterday at the Baptist church, there were prayers, believe me—prayers of thanksgiving.

You Know
What I Mean?

We're having a lot of trouble in this country lately with language, making ourselves understood. Words are the problem. They can be ambiguous sometimes. We pick a word for one of its possible meanings and somebody else hears us and applies another possible meaning. Next thing you know we're talking at cross-purposes. This happens in domestic life, as we all know. It happens in business communications, in news reporting, I can testify to that. It happens in legislation. That's why we need so many lawyers to argue about what laws are supposed to mean.

In the Clinton impeachment proceedings, we heard disputes about what sex means, what impeachment means, what an oath means, what perjury means. We even have a communication problem in the courts of the land. In the Denver, Colorado, County Court the other day, Judge Claudia Jordan sent her clerk a note. And what it said was:

Blind on right side
May be falling.
Please call someone.

Well, the clerk was quite alarmed when she read that. Her grandmother had died of a stroke and she didn't want the same thing to happen to Judge Jordan. So she called 911.

The paramedics came with a stretcher and oxygen and everything. And the judge interrupted the trial she was conducting and reassured the paramedics that she was perfectly fine. What she was trying to tell the clerk in her message was that the venetian blind on the right side of the courtroom was sagging and she was afraid it would fall down.

The paramedics weren't able to do much about that. But it just goes to show you . . . sometimes in a courtroom we get the wrong signals from witnesses, plaintiffs, the defendants, counsel . . . and sometimes from the bench.

IV.

Lab Results

The End
of Science?

At the turn of the century, according to a story that may be apocryphal, the head of the U.S. Patent Office wrote a letter to President McKinley urging that the Patent Office be shut down because, as the letter put it, "Everything that could possibly be invented has already been invented." I thought of that this morning when I saw a wire service story about science writer John Horgan's book *The End of Science,* which argues that everything important that science could possibly discover has already been discovered.

Scientists are, perhaps understandably, appalled at John Horgan's book, as I'm sure I would be miffed at a book whose title was *The End of Broadcasting.* I am absolutely certain that broadcasting is not as good as it could possibly ever get. And scientists insist that science is not as good as it's going to get, either.

But the point that Horgan seems to be making is that, in his own words, "Pure science, the quest for knowledge about what we are and where we came from, has already entered an era of diminishing returns." Horgan has attracted a lot of attention with that idea. There have been editorials in leading newspapers, interviews on public television and reports like this on radio.

The paperback rights to *The End of Science* have just been sold for an impressive $350,000, quite a lot for a science book. And in university laboratories and classrooms where science is taught and practiced, the book is so despised that you can't help but think that Horgan has touched a nerve. University of Chicago astrophysicist David Schramm calls it nonsense. He says, "I think he wanted to sell books." Well, you wouldn't have to be a rocket scientist to figure that out, but a California Institute of Technology physicist calls it fun to read in spite of its grim subject matter.

Horgan says that he's not putting science or scientists down, but he says that, in fact, they are the victims of their own success. He says, "Physicists have probed as deeply into the nature of matter as practical experiments will allow. And astronomers have seen as far into space and, therefore, into time as they ever will. And as scientists learn more and more about less and less, they're approaching unreachable limits." Biochemist Stuart Kauffman at the Santa Fe Institute calls it "well written, amusing, nasty, bitchy and entirely misleading."

No wonder it's a best-seller.

Sysnyntenoctadecanoamide

In the Journal of Science *that's just out today,*
Some researchers from Scripps Research Institute say,
That they have discovered, with the help of a cat,
A natural compound, a chemical that,
Produces a slumber, a wonderful sleep;
A sleep that's relaxing, refreshing and deep.

And they think that this substance may very well be,
In cats and in rats and in you and in me,
In the brain's spinal fluid of every mammal,
The mouse and the elephant, the dog and the camel.
Not a drug-induced sleep; it does not knock you out.
That's not what the substance they found is about.

And to think that they found such a compound as that
In the lab, with the help of a sleepy old cat!

At Scripps Research Institute they can take pride,
In Sysnyntenoctadecanoamide.

Not too catchy a name and a trifle confusing.
But that, for the nonce, is the name that they're using.
Sysnyntenoctadecanoamide.
I'm pretty sure one of these days they'll decide,
To give it a nickname more easily sung,
That rolls somewhat more trippingly off of the tongue.

They tested some cats and what they did with'm
Was to check out their sleep and circadian rhythm.
And most careful records of this they were keeping
Of a chemical found while the cats were all sleeping.
And later they saw from the records they kept
That the more of this substance the better they slept.

There was no morning after, no hangover effect
As with chemical drugs we have come to expect.
They synthesized this and injected a number
Of other lab animals and they, too, would slumber.
Not a knockout effect like barbiturate sleep,
But a sleep that was normal, refreshing and deep.

They hope to put this in a capsule someday
And see how it works, the Scripps researchers say.
It hasn't been tested on humans at all,

But those cute little pussy cats rolled in a ball,
May turn out to be quite encouraging news,
For insomniacs who cannot easily snooze.
One of these days you might sleep the night through,
Till it's time to get up, you old sleepyhead, you.

Tickle Factor

Have you ever wondered why you can't tickle yourself? It just doesn't feel the same as if someone else tickles you, even if it's in your ribs, the soles of your feet, or someplace else that's particularly ticklish. When somebody else tickles you, you squeal and giggle and squirm. When you tickle yourself, it doesn't . . . well, you know, it just doesn't . . . tickle. Well, scientists, believe it or not, have been studying this odd fact and have come up with an explanation. It's all in your head.

It's because one part of your brain tells another part of your brain, "Don't get excited, guy . . . it's just *you*." If somebody *else* is reaching out and tickling you, the message your brain gets is, "Hey . . . somebody is tickling you . . . get them to stop."

According to the journal *Nature,* neuroscience researchers, including Sarah Jane Blakemore at University College, London, got six volunteers to lie on their backs in a brain scanning machine with their eyes closed. The researchers studied the brain scan while a device with a piece of soft foam attached to a plastic rod was moved up and down to tickle the volunteers' left palms. The volunteer and the researcher took turns moving the rod so that the subjects were either tickling themselves or being tickled.

Meanwhile, the researchers were comparing activity in different parts of the brain, and concluded that the cerebellum in the lower back of the brain signals the rest of the brain what sensations to expect when you do something. When you walk, for example, it tells the brain, "We're walking now; expect pressure on the soles of the feet." If you stub your toe, the sensation is sharp and immediate. "You idiot!" your brain tells itself. "Why don't you look where you're going!?" So that's why you can't tickle yourself. And remember you heard it here first.

Warmer Thursday, Cooler Saturday

I've got a little bar bet for you. You volunteer to the person sitting next to you at the bar the information that it is warmer on weekdays than it is on weekends. "Not always, but on the average," you say. He says, "You're crazy. You don't know what you're talking about." You say, "It's true." He says, "It's not." You say, "It is so." He says, "Is not." You say, "I bet you a dollar." He says, "You're on."

And you will have made yourself a dollar, because in the northern hemisphere, Thursdays are indeed warmer than Saturdays. The fellow at the bar is not going to believe that. Who would? But you can then explain to him that the Flinders Institute of Atmospheric and Marine Sciences in Adelaide, Australia, has taken fourteen years of observations and has concluded that because of industry and the commuting that takes place during the week, the air in the lower atmosphere is, on the average, one-thirtieth of a degree warmer on weekdays than it is on weekends.

Your bar mate might not think that's much of a change, but ask an expert. Don Lenshaw of the National Center for Atmospheric Research thinks it's a big change.

DON LENSHAW: I'm surprised that the temperature change is that large, and that's part of, I think, the issue here. It seems to be larger than what one would estimate based on the amount of fuel consumption that goes on, and the differences in fuel consumption between weekdays and weekends.

OSGOOD: If it's true that weekdays are warmer than weekends, what does that tell us?

LENSHAW: It's a part of the big picture in terms of humans having an impact on the earth's climate—and the fact that sometime we're going to have to deal with these changes.

The fellow at the bar might try to argue it's just a greenhouse effect of global warming or something, but don't let him get away with that.

LENSHAW: What we're talking about here has no direct connection to climate change, because climate change is due mainly to greenhouse gases, like carbon dioxide, whereas what this would most likely be is changes due to direct fuel consumption.

The fact that one day is a bit warmer than another is not what's important, though, you tell him.

LENSHAW: It's not so much that the changes themselves have any great significance, but the fact that you can see them means that this is evidence that human activities do have a direct effect on things like the global temperature.

What *is* important, though, is that you owe me a dollar.

Good Snow–Bad Snow

There is good snow and bad snow. Good snow is the kind that makes for great skiing and snowmen. Bad snow is what falls on your front steps and your driveway. Well, we're happy to report that researchers are working hard to turn bad snow into good snow.

RUSSELL ALGIER: I like to say it's alive. It's always changing. It changes as it falls through the air. It changes once it hits the ground.

Russell Algier heads the Institute of Snow Research in Houghton, Michigan. His job is to make snow more user-friendly.

That is, to find ways to make snow do what people want it to do. And what everyone wants snow to do is to stay off the roads.

ALGIER: A new concept that we're working on is known as anti-icing, which means putting down chemicals on a highway or an airport runway before a storm. And the idea there is if we can get the chemicals on the pavement, then the snow or freezing rain that falls will tend not to stick in the first place.

Researchers are also developing a new snowmobile-trail groomer. It can create a pavement of hard snow.

ALGIER: We are looking at picking up the snow and changing it to what we want it to be. And what we want it to be is a nice hard snowmobile trail that's going to stay smooth.

The problem with fooling Mother Nature is that some things we do, such as using chemicals to remove snow, can cause other problems, such as pollution. But that just gives the engineers something else to study.

ALGIER: What the fix is, is to try and make the chemicals that we use as environmentally sound as we can possibly make them.

Unfortunately for snow researchers, the thaw in the Cold War has had a chilling effect on their budgets.

ALGIER: When I first started in this job ten years ago, there was—I guess I could get in trouble for saying this—an endless pot of money to look at any kind of military vehicle moving through snow. Lots of research going on in that area. In comparison to ten years ago, right now there's none.

Operation Desert Storm didn't help.

ALGIER: Now, if I was in sand research, I'd be in a lot better shape.

I've got a sinking feeling *that* department's going to be in business for a long time to come.

Whatever
Turns You On

We use a lot of olfactory figures of speech: "I smell a rat," "That doesn't smell right," or "The sweet smell of success." Smells affect people's moods, for better or worse. What you smell can influence how you're feeling.

DR. ALAN HIRSCH: We take it for granted, but there's an entire universe just at the tip of our nose.

We all know that pleasant smells can make life more pleasant. Our furniture smells lemony, thanks to scent in the furniture polish. We all love sniffing into a bakery when the bread's fresh out of the oven. And what they're selling at the perfume counter is, as always, hopes and dreams. But we're just beginning to realize that aromas might be used in therapeutic ways.

DR. HIRSCH: There've been a number of different studies suggesting that a green apple smell may actually reduce anxiety in normal people.

Dr. Alan Hirsch is with the Smell and Taste Treatment and Research Foundation in Chicago. Researchers there found that different scents affect our minds in different ways.

DR. HIRSCH: Lavender causes relaxation. Jasmine tends to make people more awake and alert. A mixed floral smell will make people learn faster and learn to a greater degree. Vanilla tends to make people more relaxed, reduce anxiety. Banana tends to make people sleep faster.

Some aromas don't work at all the way you'd expect. Take perfumes, for example. Research is preliminary, but studies show that perfumes generally don't put men in an amorous mood.

DR. HIRSCH: For some men who would describe that their wives or their girlfriends wore one type of perfume or another, we were able to see very small changes, but nowhere near the sort of changes that we've seen so far with cinnamon bun.

I'll repeat that—cinnamon bun. A study of male medical students found that the only aroma that got them in the mood for love was cinnamon buns.

DR. HIRSCH: If you say medical students are a reasonable approximation of other men their age in the United States, then this has potential. The only thing is that medical students could always be hungry as well, so that may have impacted upon the results, although I don't think so. One other thing is that adage, The way to a man's heart is through his stomach, might be right.

You are my little cupcake, my sweet potato pie,
My cinnamon, my honey bun. It is for you I sigh.
You're my favorite confection, so sugary and sweet.
No wonder I'm in love with you. You're good enough to eat.

Project
Woodpecker

The staff of the Lawrence Livermore National Laboratory in California has won a prize, the Intelligence Community Seal Medallion, for the terrific job they did on Project Woodpecker, but nobody is allowed to say what Project Woodpecker is. It's a secret. The folks at the laboratory are justly proud of the medallion on the wall. It means the lab did something really good. What was it? Well, let's just say it was a really good thing. To say more might compromise Project Woodpecker. What was Project Woodpecker? You're going to have to stop asking me that.

A lot of the work the lab does is like that—hush-hush. It's one of two places in the nation where nuclear weapons are designed, so Project Woodpecker might have been about that.

But then again, it might not have been. They would like to talk about the good thing they did, but they can't. Someday maybe it will be declassified and then they can tell us, but not until then.

Is the significance of the word "woodpecker" important? Was this a pecking project of some kind? No, says Ellen Fredricks, who was in charge of whatever-it-was from 1985 till 1990. She says, "At that time, we had a lot of projects with bird names." The citation that goes with the medallion on the wall is not much help, either. It says the lab tackled "a series of technical problems of enormous complexity, resulting in an extremely powerful operational capability that can be used to gather intelligence from unique sources not exploitable by any other means."

Well, if whatever-it-was was for intelligence-gathering capabilities, it means it was probably not a nuclear weapon, unless, of course, it was a nuclear weapon that could take the roof off something so we could take a look and see what was in there.

Anyway, the Lawrence Livermore Lab folks sure did a good thing, whatever it was. And so here's looking at you, kid. That was a heck of a thing you did. Keep up the good work. And whenever we think of Project Woodpecker, we'll think of you.

A New Kind
of Pen

Combining the ancient technology of the quill pen with new computer-age developments, scientists have now come up with an atomic pen that can draw a line only one-millionth of an inch thin. Who would *need* such a pen as that? President Clinton's lawyers drawing fine distinctions, perhaps? Insurance companies for limiting coverage in even smaller print that nobody could even see, much less read?

No, this new super-fine-line pen, reported in the current issue of the journal *Science,* will be used for building computer chips a thousand times smaller than the ones now used in computers. Chemistry professor Chad A. Mirkin and his colleagues at Northwestern University have learned how to draw a line 15 nanometers wide. A nanometer is one-billionth of a meter. A fine human hair is about 10,000 nanometers thick. Using a stylus or pen tip made of silicon nitride, and an atomic force microscope, this pen can lay down silver or copper a few molecules at a time, to create an electronic circuit chip. A teeny-weeny itty-bitty chip. I know that doesn't sound real scientific, but these lines are so thin that a million could be squeezed into one inch. That means extremely powerful and extremely sophisticated computers can one day be built that are no bigger than your laptop.

They say the pen is mightier than the sword. This one is, that's for sure. It's expensive as pens go—but when it comes to the fine lines of nano-technology, the Duchess of Windsor's rule applies: You can't be too rich . . . or too thin.

Progress?

Have you noticed that some of the things that are supposed to speed you up and make your life easier actually slow you down and make life harder? Well, I have. Admittedly, with computers and e-mail and cell phones and fax machines and all that stuff, things are possible now that weren't possible before, but we didn't miss them because we didn't know about them. Now that we have all these things, try to use them productively to organize our lives better, we find ourselves so dependent on them that they're beginning to rule our lives and snow us under with too much information, which is not what we had in mind when we bought the darn things.

Here's a new word for you: the verb "recomplicate." Instead of simplifying your life the way you want electronic digital marvels to do, they've actually given you more stuff to worry about. Ten or so years ago, before I had a computer, a cell phone, a pager, a fax machine, a digital answering machine and a personal copier in the house, things were simpler, I think. The telephone would ring and you'd answer it. If nobody was home, nobody would answer it, and whoever was calling would have to call you back.

If you wanted to send somebody a letter, you wrote it, put it in an envelope, put a stamp on it and put it in the mailbox, and a couple of days later, it would show up in somebody else's mailbox. The word "mailbox" in those day meant literally a box in which the mailman (that's what carriers used to be called) would put your mail.

There would be bills in there, of course, but there would also be letters from people you actually knew and postcards from friends on vacation. You would check this box once a day with pleasure. Now what's in there mostly is junk mail and bills. It's your e-mailbox that contains the good stuff. But you're supposed to check that every few minutes.

Jeff Davidson, the author of a book titled *Breathing Space: Living and Working at a Comfortable Pace in a Sped-Up Society,* says, "You name me a technology and I'll tell you the flip side." In the old days, you did not run out of toner. You didn't know what toner was. You kept typing until the ribbon had holes in it. But today, people hire professional organizers to help them cut through the jungle of complexity made possible by all these technological improvements.

Technological improvement is getting out of hand.
I've got just about as much improvement now as I can stand.

Armored
Car Doors

New patent figures show that for the first time since 1985, the U.S. Patent Office issued more patents to Americans last year than to Japanese. It's good to see the United States getting back into the inventiveness lead. There are some things that need improving, and they're not all high-tech, either.

For example, wouldn't you think somebody would come up with an improved rear door for armored cars? The armored car rear doors that they have now are not very good, if the news reports are any indication. It seems armored car doors keep springing open, spilling incredible amounts of money onto the highways and byways of America. It happens all the time.

Just the other night in Detroit, it happened again. It seems a money bag inside an armored truck fell against the door latch, pushing it open. And four large bags of money and food stamps spilled out onto the street. And passersby went bananas. Of the $1.7 million that spilled onto the street, only $7,000 has been recovered.

The Guardian Armored Securities vehicle went a few blocks after its rear door popped open. The driver and guards didn't realize what had happened until a pedestrian flagged them down and told them.

Meanwhile, back at the Hilton Supermarket, people were running in with their arms loaded with cash, checks and food stamps, stuffing them into grocery bags and going out with them. Motorists were pulling off to the side or stopping right out in the middle of the street and gathering some of the money that was blowing around. "It was pandemonium," says one eye-witness.

It only took a few minutes for the truck to get back to the place where its doors had sprung open, but by then the only thing left of the four big bags that had fallen out was one small pouch that had been in one of the larger bags.

People are not at their best when there are millions of dollars all over the street. Changing human nature is going to be difficult, if not impossible. But improving the armored car rear doors so they won't keep popping open at inopportune times should be doable, one would think.

My car has a display on the dash that tells me when a door is open. It even shows which one. You'd think a car built to carry millions of dollars would have at least that much. And do the doors on your car keep springing open all the time? Mine don't, either. Why do they make armored car doors that seem to pop open if you look at them cross-eyed? I don't know.

But some inventor who invents a better armored car rear door is going to make—you should excuse the expression—a windfall.

The National
Pothole System

Every winter it gets cold and then colder and then not so cold, and things freeze and then they thaw and then they freeze again. And below the lovely blanket that covers so much of the United States at that time, something is stirring. Mother Nature is at work, creating that perennial phenomenon we all know so well—the pothole.

Everybody hates potholes. We certainly hate hitting potholes. You're driving along, blissfully unaware of what's waiting for you just ahead, and suddenly, bang—a message from your front end. Sometimes it's nothing more than that, but now and then your hubcap rolls away, somehow attaining a faster speed than you and in a different direction. Sometimes your tire goes, sometimes your axle. I hate it when that happens, don't you?

The only people who love potholes are the tire dealers and the front-end specialists.

At such times we say to ourselves, "Why? If we can put a man on the moon, if we can split the atom, if we can splice genes, if we can conquer static cling, why cannot we surface our roads with something that doesn't turn into Swiss cheese if you look at it cross-eyed?"

If modern technology can send my voice through the air and into a car radio at the speed of light, surely it can find some material that's better than what we use now to pave the roads with. No offense intended. I surely don't want to get any asphalt or concrete contractors mad at me, but this is ridiculous.

The surface of the upper level of the George Washington Bridge, so painfully restored, a couple of months later resembles the surface of the moon. After I hit a big pothole the other night, my wife, Jean, said, "Why did you do that? Why didn't you just drive around it?" "Well, you can't just drive around something like that," I explained. "You've got to stay in your lane. If everybody on the bridge was trying to drive around the potholes, it would be even more like bumper tag than it already is."

Potholes are a major pain in the neck, and yet I noticed that the president in his State of the Union address did not mention potholes even once. When, I ask you, is this country going to wake up and come to grips with, yes, the pothole crisis?

The Mouse
That Roared

It's been said that if you build a better mousetrap, the world will beat a pathway to your door. And in Indiana a chemist has invented a better mousetrap—well, not a trap exactly, but a way to encourage mice to go beat a pathway to somebody else's door.

There are many ways homeowners deal with mice. They can, for example, get themselves a cat or two.

MILOSH NOVOTONY: Most of the time, they do a pretty good job in keeping mice away. Some people don't like cats, I guess, or are allergic to cats. Then, the other alternative is to have the mousetraps. It's—it's messy and perhaps somewhat inhumane. And then, of course, another one is to poison them. And that, again, has its drawbacks.

Milosh Novotony thought that there had to be a better solution. And so the chemistry professor at Indiana University started experimenting with farnesenes. Those are the odors that mice excrete in urine. Dominant male mice use it to mark their territory. It's their way of saying, "I'm the big guy around here, and don't mess with me."

NOVOTONY: Then the other mice are reluctant to enter the area because they fear the strong, dominant mouse.

Novotony was able to artificially synthesize this essence of male mouse and found it made an excellent mouse repellent. Male mice stayed away. They figured there was a big, mean, aggressive mouse living in there. True, a few female mice apparently found the scent alluring.

NOVOTONY: But most of the time, even the female mice would hesitate.

Novotony has patented the chemical. He's now looking for a manufacturer to produce it as an aerosol spray or perhaps a pellet that could be placed around the house. The aroma, he says, is quite pleasant.

NOVOTONY: Kind of more reminiscent of plant materials like leaves and pine needles and that sort of thing.

This is a product that could be loved by animal-rights activists.

NOVOTONY: It's your typical green product. That means it doesn't kill the animals; it would just mentally send them to your neighbor.

Your neighbor, of course, might not appreciate that very much. But, as Novotony points out, that's not your problem.

NOVOTONY: He has got a problem, so he better get some of that spray, too.

Strange-Looking
Objects

It's amazing the things that, for better or worse, the human imagination can devise. What would you do if, quite unexpectedly, a suspicious-looking box showed up on your doorstep, swathed in tape and held together with rubber bands? Think about that. And if you were managing a supermarket and found out that $30 hams had been mistakenly advertised at $5, what would you do to try to rectify the situation? And if your life depended on it, could you figure out what to do with a paring knife with a propeller attached, or a vibrating sunflower? Do ideas spring to your mind?

Well, let's see, where shall we start? How about the vibrating "Dynamic Sunflower," as inventor Jonathan Sheiffes calls it. It won him $3,220 in prizes at the Malmose Flugelminder

Challenge in London. Malmose is a British company that makes the so-called lava lamps. They sponsor this contest every year to find the world's most weird but workable invention. The Dynamic Sunflower meets the test in that it is weird and it does work. It's bright yellow like a sunflower, positioned inside a blue bowl covered with flashing lights, and it does vibrate. Sheiffes says its purpose is as a substitute for an open fire.

The little onion fan knife was another entry. It's designed for use when chopping an onion to blow away the fumes so that the chopper's eyes won't water.

The $30 hams advertised at $5 were a problem not too smoothly handled by a supermarket in Cleveland, as a co-owner of the market acknowledges. Employees went around the store grabbing hams out of the arms and shopping carts of customers. Two women complained that the meat manager grabbed the hams back so forcefully that their hands were bruised and scratched. One shopper complained that a store official used a racial slur while grabbing her ham; not her ham actually, but the one she was carrying.

Finally, the suspicious box that was held together with tape and rubber bands and arrived at a man's doorstep in Lubbock, Texas. The man gingerly carried the box to his backyard and then called the police. The bomb squad came and removed the box to a vacant lot and ever so carefully opened it up. There were no wires or batteries in there; no explosives. What was in there was a chocolate pie. Why, what did you think it was?

V

Osgood's
Health
Tips

Osgood Health Tip #1:
Artificial Flavorings

Although Osgood health tips have my name on them, I do not make them up, although they often sound like something I might have made up. Right now I want to tell you about a new study which suggests that we are all better off and healthier because of all the artificial flavorings we've taken in over the last several years.

Yes, friends, if this study, done at the National Center for Health Statistics, holds up, these artificial flavorings in everything from toothpaste to barbecue potato chips may not be so terrible for you. In fact, they may actually be good for you. I know that for years you've been hearing people say that processed foods with artificial flavorings in them are bad for you. But at a conference in San Francisco sponsored by the

American Heart Association, two researchers from the National Center for Health Statistics in Hyattsville, Maryland, Dr. Manning Feinlieb and Lillian M. Ingster, presented some evidence that America's taste for artificial flavorings of all kinds may help explain why starting about thirty years ago, fewer of us have been dying of heart attacks.

That's not to say that some other factors may have played a role, such as less cigarette smoking now, lower consumption of saturated fats, some better medicines, more exercise, but the heart attacks started going down before we started doing all that stuff. And the hypothesis presented by Ingster and Feinlieb is that artificial flavorings used in baked goods, soda pop, candy, chewing gum, ketchup, ice cream, puddings, mouthwash, toothpaste and so on, especially fake strawberry, fake grape, fake butter, fake vanilla, fake cinnamon, fake mint, fake caramel and fake walnut all contain salicylate, a chemical cousin of aspirin, which is acetylsalicylic acid. Aspirin is known to prevent blood clots and so reduce the risk of heart attacks.

Salicylates in artificial flavorings, according to Dr. Feinlieb, may be the missing link in explaining why this decline in heart attacks occurred when it did. There's enough salicylate in the artificial flavoring an ordinary American takes in to give you the equivalent of one baby aspirin per day, about 80 milligrams, which is the dosage recommended, especially for older people, as a way of warding off heart attacks. I'm not saying you should load up on junk food, but this has been another Osgood health tip, all of which should be taken with a pinch of salt and maybe a little strawberry salicylate.

Discovering
the Obvious

Sometimes scientific studies are done to discover something that everybody already knew. The way to lose weight is to diet and exercise; everybody knows that. But most people, as soon as they go off their diet and stop the exercise, put the weight they took off right back on again.

You do not have to be Sherlock Holmes to figure out why this happens or what you have to do to keep it from happening. But a project carried out by the National Weight Control Registry, the University of Pittsburgh and the University of Colorado was reported to a meeting of the North American Association for the Study of Obesity. And after carefully studying 786 people who lost an average of sixty-six pounds and managed to keep it off, they have come up, finally, with the secret of what these people do that's different than the people who lose the weight and put it right back on.

Most overweight people can lose weight by going on a diet and starting a regular exercise program. They don't take in so much fat and so many calories when they eat and they burn up more fat and calories when they exercise. But then, when they stop dieting and stop exercising, they go right back to being just as fat as they were, sometimes fatter.

But some people, including the 786 people studied by Dr. Mary Clemm of the University of Pittsburgh and a team of researchers at the University of Colorado, managed to avoid putting all the weight back on when they stopped dieting and exercising by the simple expedient of not stopping.

So here was the big revelation at the North American Association for the Study of Obesity meeting: If you want to take off the weight, diet and exercise. If you want to keep it off, which is the problem most of us have, then keep dieting and exercising. Isn't that what you already thought? Well, that's what I thought you already thought.

So science marches on, discovering yet again something everybody already knew. It is, however, a perfect illustration of Osgood's First Law, which is: Just because something is obvious doesn't necessarily mean that science isn't going to discover it tomorrow. And just because we know what we ought to be doing doesn't necessarily mean that we're going to do it.

Miraculous Disease
Prevention
Procedure Discovered

The Commonwealth of Massachusetts, home to the Harvard Medical School, MIT, hundreds of medical centers and independent research labs doing work on the leading edge of medical technology, has announced a new program that could dramatically reduce the spread of infection.

Nationally, the doctors say, the WYH procedure advocated by this program could spare millions of Americans from getting sick with colds, flu, Hepatitis A, eye infections, dysentery and a host of other nasty illnesses. The procedure is one that does not involve lasers or nuclear medicine or radiation or gene splicing or any such thing. You can do it yourself at home. All the WYH procedure requires is soap and water. WYH stands for Wash Your Hands. But believe it or not, most people don't do it often enough or do it right.

How long does it take you to wash your hands? Ten seconds? Fifteen or twenty seconds? No good, says Dr. Bela Matyas of the Massachusetts Department of Public Health. Just passing your hands under running water isn't anywhere near good enough. To wash your hands correctly, the doctor says, takes at least thirty seconds to a minute or more.

Before officially launching a two-year campaign featuring a cartoon character named Soapy, Massachusetts Medical Society officials sprinkled some white powder—synthetic germs—on the hands of several observers. About a half an hour later, ultraviolet lights highlighted traces of that powder everywhere—on clothes and pens and hair and chairs and faces. Dr. Joseph Heyman, the president of the society, says people don't realize where their hands are going.

Each year an estimated 40 million Americans get sick from the bacteria transmitted by dirty hands. And no wonder! Last year researchers studying the bathroom habits of more than six thousand men and women in five American cities found that only 74 percent of the women and only 61 percent of the men bothered to wash their hands at all after using the toilet. It does not take a scientific genius to know that this is spreading disease, especially since most of the people who *are* washing their hands aren't doing it right. You wouldn't think, would you, that these days it would be necessary to point out what your mama tried to tell you all those years? WYH! Wash your hands!

Osgood Health
Tip #2: Cholesterol

Part of you wants your cholesterol level to be low. That's the part of you that knows about the relationship between high cholesterol levels and cardiovascular disease and doesn't want to die of a heart attack. But would you believe there is a part of you that doesn't want your cholesterol level low and makes you feel sad when it is low? A new French study says that low cholesterol may lead to depression and even suicide.

I remember a song from my youth, the first two lines of which were: "Black-strap molasses and wheat-germ bread make you feel so good, you'll wish you were dead." Silly as those words may be, they came to mind this morning when I read about this new study done at the National Institute of Health and Medical Research in Paris. They've monitored the cholesterol levels of six thousand working men over a period of seventeen years and discovered that there is a correlation between low cholesterol and depression and suicide; and between declining cholesterol and suicide. In other words, according to the *British Medical Journal,* in which the study results were published, there is something about lowering your cholesterol, however good it may be for your arteries, that makes you want to kill yourself. It makes you feel so good, you'll wish you were dead.

In another study at the University of Vienna, it was found that the cholesterol levels of twenty pregnant women dropped sharply right away as soon as their babies were born. This does happen. The doctors there found what they call a significant correlation between a decrease in cholesterol and depressive symptoms. Could it be that so-called postpartum depression is caused not by parting with the baby but by parting with the cholesterol?

Cholesterol may be inversely proportional to health, but apparently it's directly proportional to mood. So what do you want to be, happy or alive? Evidently you can't have it both ways.

Disorder of the Month — BDD

Is there something about your appearance that you think makes you look ugly? I'm not talking about needing to lose a little weight or get yourself a new hairstyle. I'm talking about some part of your body you can't do much about, but which you think is horrible although nobody else seems to notice.

But you can't get it out of your head that your nose may be— or your skin or your head may be—as ugly as sin. Well, possibly you are suffering from a new disorder I just found out about. Well, it's not really new, I'm sure, but it has been newly identified and classified. It is called BDD, for Body Dismorphic Disorder. Some British psychiatrists are complaining that doctors aren't doing enough to help people suffering from BDD. In an article in the *British Journal of Psychiatry*, Dr. David Veal of Groveland Priority Hospital in London writes that some people become so distressed over a deformity that's so slight hardly anybody would even notice, or that in some cases doesn't even exist at all, that they become clinically depressed and sometimes even kill themselves. Dr. Veal says of the fifty people with Body Dismorphic Disorder that he has treated, 25 percent have tried to kill themselves.

In the mind of someone with BDD, an imaginary defect can become a literally fatal flaw. Veal says 40 percent never mention their concerns to their doctors because they're afraid the doctors wouldn't understand. And they're right, says Veal. BDD, he says, is a chronic handicapping disorder, and patients are not being adequately identified or treated by health professionals. In fact, he says of those who did tell their doctors about it, 83 percent were unhappy with the response they got.

"Doctor, I hate my chin. My chin is so ugly, so deformed that it makes me sick even thinking about it." And the doctor would most likely say something like, "What are you talking about? There's nothing the matter with your chin." Now to say something like that to a BDD sufferer who thinks his chin is so ugly he might want to kill himself does no good whatsoever. He thinks people are lying to him when they tell him that his chin is okay. That makes him feel even worse. I mean, it's bad enough having such a grotesque chin without having people lie to you about it!

So yet another syndrome or disorder to add to today's catalog of exotic illnesses.

If you think your nose
Is like something that grows

In the rot on the stump of a tree,
It is true, I suppose,
You might have a bad nose—
But you may only have BDD.
If that's what it was
You don't need a new schnoz,
You need something different instead.
The problem's not there right in front of your face.
The problem is inside your head.

Osgood Health
Tip #3: Laughter

L aughter may not be the best medicine, as *Reader's Digest* always claimed, but it is medicine. Now comes word from London, where the annual meeting of the British Psychological Society is going on, that there's a new study showing that laughter is, indeed, good for you. It seems to stimulate the body's immune system. Furthermore, social drinkers tend to laugh more than people who drink very little alcohol or none at all. This would suggest that drinking might also be good for you, an Osgood health tip if ever there was one.

Look around you at the Christmas party and you may well observe that people are laughing more than they do, let's say, standing around the office elevator or around the water cooler.

And those who are imbibing a little Christmas cheer seem to be laughing more than those who are not. Well, this same observation has been made by Jeffrey Lowe, a psychologist at the University of Hull, who told the annual meeting of the British Psychological Society not that the more alcohol you drink, the more fun you'll have and the more healthy you'll be; that is certainly not the case.

"We're saying," says Lowe, "that perhaps people shouldn't use alcohol as a medicine but only as a facilitator for fun, and I believe that might be the important thing, unlike the earlier biological and medical studies which suggested that alcohol has a cardiological protective effect. Our message is that maybe it has something to do with a person's lifestyle and attitude to life and the fact that they engage in fun and laughter more."

Moderate drinkers laugh more. The more you laugh, the better. As far as your immune system is concerned, that is true. But it is not true that the more you drink, the more you laugh. Lowe says females tend to drink less than males, but they don't necessarily laugh less. The tie between the laughing and the good health is much stronger than the tie between the drinking and the laughing.

What Lowe and his colleagues did to study all this, I swear, was to visit pubs. They did so entirely in the line of duty, of course, not to have a good time, perish the thought. Their sole purpose was to observe other people having a good time. Or not such a good time, as the case might be. Then they tried a controlled lab experiment where they sat volunteers down to watch a funny film and gave them either alcohol or soft drinks. Trained observers counted the laughs, and again, those given the alcohol tended to laugh more. Why? They don't know. "All we can say at the moment," says Dr. Lowe, "is that there is a link."

What is the moral, then? To drink more? "I wouldn't necessarily drink more based on this research," says Lowe. "I would laugh more."

Are you laughing? Good.

Times, Days and Seasons to Avoid

You can get a heart attack any time of the day or night. But do you know what the most likely time is? Right about now! Early in the morning when you first get up. Just climbing out of bed raises blood pressure, spikes stress hormones and makes the blood stickier.

There are several new reports tracking which seasons, which hours of the day and days of the week a heart attack is most likely to attack, or a stroke is most likely to strike.

Statistics can tell us when heart attacks happen most. Why they happen when they do is what cardiologists are trying to figure out. You and I can guess, but our guesses are likely to be wrong. For example, heart attacks happen more often on Mondays than any other day of the week. Aha! you say.

Obviously, that's because everybody has to go back to work on Monday. But not everybody has to. Retired people don't have to go to work on Monday. Yet the research shows that even retired people are more likely to have heart attacks on Mondays.

And heart attacks are far more likely in the wintertime than they are in the summertime. I know what you're thinking. You're thinking it's the cold weather that's to blame, people having to bundle up, having to shovel the snow off their driveways. It figures that people would have more heart attacks in the winter. But then how do you explain the seasonal rise in the number of winter heart attacks in Los Angeles where you don't have to bundle up and where it never snows? Yet L.A. heart attacks climb sharply around Thanksgiving, peak at New Year's and January is the worst.

Could it be the holidays? A little too much celebrating, eating and drinking, perhaps?

As for time of day: the nighttime is when you are least likely to have a heart attack. However, if you *do* have one at night, that's when you're most likely to *die.*

For various reasons we can't avoid seasons,
Or hours or days as you know.
Although dreaded by some all these things simply come.
And sometimes when they come . . . we go.

A Real
Stress Test

Stress can bring on a heart attack; there's no question about that. But there are different kinds of stress. And a new study at Duke University suggests that mental stress tests might be better indicators of who's likely to have a heart attack than the treadmill test everybody now uses. Mental stress testing, they say, could include solving complex math problems on a tight deadline or something most people find very stressful indeed: public speaking.

Now far be it from me to question the recommendations of the good doctors at Duke University, but I happen to know that in order to test somebody by having them make a speech before an audience, you need to have an audience. The presence of an audience is what causes the stress. But who are you going to get to sit there and listen to somebody's speech which he's only making to find out how likely he is to have a heart attack? How would you recruit such an audience? Have people write in for tickets, round people up off the street the way they do here in New York for the TV talk shows? The idea of having people do public speaking as an alternative to running on a treadmill as suggested in the Duke University study does not deal with the question of how you get an audience to sit still and listen to such a speech. But I'll tell you, I would hate to be the one who had to round up the audience for it.

I have what seems to me a somewhat more practical suggestion for something that would produce at least as much stress and not require the participation of a whole crowd of people. What you do is, you wire the patient up with electrodes and everything, same as you would for a treadmill test or presumably for a public speaking test, and then—now this would require the cooperation of the federal government, to some extent, but surely this could be arranged—you bring in a guy carrying a briefcase and introduce him as an agent of the Internal Revenue Service, who will now conduct an audit of your income tax returns for the years 1989 through 1994. Then, as you answer the IRS agent's questions about your deductions and expenses and where your receipts are and everything, the doctors can be monitoring your electrocardiogram, or whatever else they've got you hooked up to. Now that is what I call a stress test!

My experience over the years has taught me that it's a heck of a lot easier to round up an IRS man than an audience, and they're just as hard to please.

Osgood Health
Tip #4: Sugar

As you regular listeners know, we are very health-conscious here on "The Osgood Files." And although we are profoundly unqualified to discuss such topics as nutrition and medicine, we do so all the time. If I was afraid to comment on the subject simply because I didn't know the first thing about it, what sort of a broadcast commentator would I be?

Our Osgood health tip today is based on a study published in an issue of *The New England Journal of Medicine,* a Vanderbilt University study which says if your little kids are normal, you can feed them candy bars, soda pop and other stuff with sugar, and it won't make them hyperactive or otherwise adversely affect their behavior.

We normally suggest that you take our Osgood health tips with a grain of salt. Today, however, a grain of sugar might be more appropriate. For some time now, a lot of parents have believed that it was sugar that was to blame if their kids were cranky or distracted or bouncing off the walls. Some studies were done in which children would be given some soda pop and candy bars and then about five minutes later, somebody would follow the kids around and write down everything they did. That somewhat muddy procedure is how they decided that sugar made children hyperactive.

Well, what they did in this study at Vanderbilt University, according to *The New England Journal of Medicine,* was to go to the homes of twenty-five normal preschoolers, aged three to five, and to the homes of twenty-three kids six to ten years old who had been described by their parents as being sensitive to sugar. Dietitians took all the food out of their homes and left behind prepared meals for them and their families.

Over a nine-week period, the families followed three different diets, each one lasting three weeks. One of those diets used sugar, another aspartame—that's NutraSweet—and the other one used saccharine. Now, these families had no way in the world of knowing which one they were getting at any given time. And the kids certainly weren't sure when they were switched from one regimen to another.

Throughout all this, the children were watched and tested to see if there were any changes, and there were some in some cases, but some kids' behavior actually improved when they were on the sugar diet. Dr. March Woolrich of Vanderbilt, who ran the study, says, "There is no evidence sugar has an adverse effect on children's behavior." And he says the same thing is true of aspartame, by the way.

The bottom line is that studies are muddy, but candy is dandy.

Cutting Us
Some Slack

Every religion has rules—certain things you must or must not do, but most ministers of religion realize that people are not perfect, that the faithful are not always so faithful. So in church there are the concepts of forgiveness and redemption for the prodigal son or daughter. However, up to now, the high priests of health, the ones who write the rules for what you should or shouldn't eat, for example, have not exactly been models of tolerance. If you eat a breakfast of buttered toast, bacon and eggs, they've pretty much suggested you may as well go jump off a tall building or play a little game of Russian roulette.

But now comes the American Heart Association with some reduced-guilt guidelines that take into consideration how human we humans are.

We are our own worst enemies, as anyone can see.
We don't act as we know we should. What fools we mortals be!
We know the things we should not eat, I think it's safe to say,
But nonetheless, when tempted to, we eat them anyway.
And that's the way it is with us. The human situation
Is that we can resist anything except, of course, temptation.
And when we stray and eat, let's say, a hamburger surprise,
We feel so bad we also add an order of cheese fries.
And since we've been so terrible, how much more could it hurt
To have it with a milk shake and a nice, gooey dessert?

Such is the mind of humankind. Our willpower is weak.
On this I am an expert and I know whereof I speak.
So I was rather pleased to see the guidelines out today
From the Heart Association, the respected AHA.
The recommended maximum of cholesterol and fat
Hasn't been changed; oh no, they aren't giving up on that.
But if one day you chance to stray, as sometimes we all do,
Well, now they say you'll be okay if, the next day or two,
You go back to the regimen you know darn well you should.
If you've been bad, in other words, go back to being good.

The new AHA guidelines out today have been revamped
To let us know effects of eating badly can be damped
By going back to eating right as quickly as we can,
Since perfection isn't one of the known qualities of man.
And if you slip a little now, they say, don't give up hope,
For perfection means too steep and far too slippery a slope.
For the Heart Association, a more realistic tack:
Since we are the way we are, to cut us just a little slack.

Shopping

One of the ways in which women and men tend to be different from one another is that most women love to go shopping. They actually get pleasure from hours at a crowded shopping mall. Men would just as soon have root canal.

Now from Britain, all dressed up in scientific wrappings, comes proof that for such men shopping in crowded stores raises stress levels to the point where it's hazardous to their health.

British psychologist David Lewis, who did the study on men's stress levels while Christmas shopping, says, "The peak stress levels were equivalent to emergency situations experienced by fighter pilots or policemen going into dangerous situations."

This is probably *not* what the people at the Brent Cross Shopping Center in North London, who commissioned the study, were hoping to hear. But Lewis sent three dozen men and women of different ages to stores with identical Christmas lists. Each shopper was accompanied by a researcher who recorded periodic blood pressure and heart rate. They found that one out of four women had elevated heart and blood pressure rates, but every single man in the study had significant increases. Even before they stepped out the front door to head for the stores, more than 70 percent of them started to show these symptoms. Lewis says, "For men even the thought of going shopping was enough to send stress levels soaring!"

Most of the men, when queried, admitted that they were likely to choose the first gift they'd see rather than spend any more time in the stores than they absolutely had to. They couldn't get out of there fast enough. Some women brought husbands or boyfriends along. And most of the ones who did so admitted later that they wish they'd left them at home. The stress levels for women with men along were much higher than for those who went alone or brought their kids with them.

Some stores play cheery music to make everybody feel good. The survey indicates that, for men anyway, the loud cheery music made them feel *worse*.

To each his own, they often say.
And his own to each.
But for men the expression "Shop till you drop"
May be more than a figure of speech.

Osgood Health Tip #5:
Don't Lick Golf Balls

There are some things you'd think you wouldn't have to warn people to do or not to do. A while back, there was a campaign to get people to make sure when they put eye drops in their eyes that they weren't picking up the wrong container and putting glue in their eyes instead. You would think people would know not to put glue in their eyes.

I told you about a big campaign in Massachusetts to get people to wash their hands. It is amazing how many people don't wash their hands when they go to the bathroom or before they prepare food or sit down to eat. Their mothers told them to wash their hands, no doubt, but nobody's told them recently.

And now, an Osgood health tip for you golfers: When you're

out on the golf course, do not lick your golf ball. Some people do, apparently, with the idea that the golf ball will travel faster. My health tip is: Never do that.

In the new issue of the British Medical Association's journal, *Guts,* Dr. Connor Burke warns that you can get really sick licking your golf balls. Dr. Burke, of the James Connolly Memorial Hospital in Dublin, describes the case of one sixty-five-year-old golfer who used to lick his golf ball clean before teeing off all the time. He came down with hepatitis, even though he is a non-drinker and doesn't have any of the other habits that are normally associated with hepatitis.

It turned out that the golf course he played on regularly used the exfoliant Agent Orange to control weeds, and he was taking in Agent Orange every time he licked the ball. When he stopped licking the golf balls, the hepatitis went away. He still didn't believe it had anything to do with his golf ball licking, but when he resumed doing it again, the hepatitis came back. So now he's a believer and carries a damp cloth with him to wipe the ball.

Admittedly, I do not know the first thing about hepatitis or about golf either, for that matter. But I am perfectly willing to take Dr. Burke's warning at face value. And so today's Osgood health tip is: Do not clean your golf balls with your tongue. I would have mentioned this before, but I never thought the subject would come up.

Crime and Punishment

VI.

Smooth Operators

Bank robbery has always attracted certain criminal minds because, as Willie Sutton explained when asked why he robbed banks, "That's where the money is."

Sutton kept robbing banks and getting caught and sent to prison and escaping and robbing more banks and getting caught again and sent to prison again. He was clever enough to escape but not clever enough to get into some other line of work.

Harry Houdini, who had some of Sutton's gifts, made a good living in show business. The secret of a well-staged act or prison break is planning, thinking everything through, anticipating every step, patient rehearsal to get your moves and your timing down right. All of this was sadly lacking in the bank robbery recently in West Covina, California, near Los Angeles.

Four men entered the Wells Fargo Bank branch there with guns drawn and ordered everyone to get down on the floor. One of the robbers was bleeding, apparently having somehow managed to shoot himself before walking into the bank, which is a poor start for a bank robbery no matter what else you do right. In fact, they did not do much else right.

These particular bank robbers, not wanting to get stuck with marked bills or with exploding dye packs, grabbed a cartful of coins instead. The disadvantage of coins is that they usually come in much smaller denominations than bills do and they're much heavier and they're much more difficult to carry around. In this case, as the robbers rolled the cartful of coins onto the sidewalk, it tipped over and coins spilled out all over the place.

These were not what Willie Sutton would have called smooth operators. The police later were able to find the first getaway van by following the trail of blood that the wounded bank robber left behind. And when they got out of the van and into a second car, witnesses noted their suspicious demeanor and wrote down the license number of the second vehicle. This made it a lot easier for the authorities to solve the case and to find and arrest the alleged perpetrators.

Says police lieutenant Wayne Heieck, "Talk about dumb and dumber. Somebody could write a screenplay about this puppy."

Canterbury Tale

This is the story of fifty-one-year-old Charles Barry of Canterbury, New Hampshire, who is being sent to prison because he doesn't have cancer.

Barry, a car salesman for Grappone Auto Junction in Concord, went to his boss and told him that he needed to be put on a part-time schedule because he was dying of cancer—kidney, lung and prostate cancer. The boss did put Barry on a part-time schedule, but he sent him his full paycheck every week. His former wife and three stepsons felt sorry for him.

Everybody felt sorry for Charles Barry. You had to feel sorry for someone who was having seizures, whose head was shaved, who used to talk about how awful it was to be undergoing chemotherapy. At the United Community Church in Canterbury, where he served as a deacon, he addressed the congregation and told them to use him as an example of how to live with adversity. The church took up a collection for him. Another church gave him money, too. Friends and neighbors chipped in thousands of dollars. It was all very sad about Charles.

But in truth, Charles Barry didn't have cancer at all. For six years, he faked having cancer. He pretended to have seizures, batting his head against the wall sometimes to be more convincing. He would drop red dye in the toilet to make it look like there was blood in his urine. It was all a scam.

The people who gave him money were acting out of kindness. They might have given it to some worthy cause otherwise. In any event, a former girlfriend got suspicious and went to prosecutors, and it was quickly established that Barry had no real symptoms of cancer whatsoever.

He is not somebody who was misdiagnosed. He is not a hypochondriac, somebody who thought he had cancer. "He's a con man," says federal prosecutor Arnold Huftalen.

Barry pleaded guilty to fraud charges, and he was given the maximum sentence by U.S. District Judge Ernest Torres. Charles Barry must serve fourteen months in prison, he must do two hundred hours of community service, and he has been ordered to repay some $43,000 to his victims, including the car dealer employer to whom he had sold a bill of goods and to the churches and friends and neighbors and other good people in Canterbury. At his sentencing, Barry apologized. "What I did was very awful. I just want to say I'm sorry," he said. Nobody feels sorry for Charles Barry now. They used to, but not anymore.

The Negotiator

People who get into the burglary business apparently do so because they're not very good at making money the old-fashioned, legal way. Robert Jones made off with jewelry, credit cards and a cell phone from a private home . . . and then negotiated it all away. Jones is apparently a better burglar than he is a negotiator.

At three o'clock in the morning—and I can tell you from years of personal experience that three o'clock in the morning is the middle of the night—Stanley Seewald and his wife were awakened by the sound of an intruder in their home in Brooklyn, New York. Seewald got up, encountered the burglar and struggled with him. The man ran out the back door, taking with him some costume jewelry, credit cards . . . and Seewald's cellular phone.

When the police arrived, they found and followed footprints in the new-fallen snow. Meanwhile Seewald tried to call the burglar on the cell phone. He dialed the number several times and each time somebody would answer, say hello, and then hang up. Finally, Seewald got him to stay on the line long enough to say that he needed the phone and would buy it back from the burglar. The burglar said he wanted $200 for it. Seewald said he only paid $179 for it brand-new. A hundred fifty, the man said. How about a hundred? Finally, Seewald got him down to $80. They agreed to meet. Then, along with two cops, Seewald went to the agreed meeting spot. The suspect, Robert Jones, came over to the van with the cell phone, and before he knew what hit him he was under arrest.

One of the cops recognized Jones. He had arrested him once before. Seewald got all his stuff back. As for the hapless Mr. Jones, he's charged with burglary, robbery and criminal possession of stolen property. Looking back on it, Jones must realize that he did something wrong there. The burglary itself went well enough. But the negotiating part was where things went sour.

Always an Explanation

There's always an explanation for why people behave strangely. Why was the man in Windsor, Connecticut, pulling twenty-dollar bills out of his underwear and throwing them out a car window? Why was the man in Mound Bayou, Mississippi, running as fast as his legs could carry him and rolling a tire alongside him as he ran? And why were the people waiting on line at the Wells Fargo Bank in Riverside, California, so horrified to see the police come in and arrest two extortion suspects? I can explain everything.

The reason the man was taking twenty-dollar bills out of his underwear and throwing them out the window of a car in Windsor, Connecticut, was that the car was a police car and Kenneth Lunn was being taken to the station house for booking on bank robbery charges, and he started coughing and asked the police officers to roll the window down. And when they did, he reached into his shorts and grabbed the bills and threw them out onto I-91. The cops had to scramble to scoop up the unexpected cash flow, which Lunn must have figured was evidence that might be used against him. He is being held on bank robbery charges.

As for Robert Johnson, the man in Mound Bayou, Mississippi? He was described by Police Chief Richard Crowe as "the fastest runner I've ever seen of somebody rolling a tire." He had been inflating the tire at a service station when somebody spotted what looked like drugs in the tire. Chief Crowe showed up; Robert Johnson and the tire took off. At some point, he must have noticed that the tire was leaving a trail through the weeds, and so he left the tire behind and it was recovered with six pounds of marijuana inside. Johnson was subsequently tracked down with the help of dogs. Things haven't changed much in Mound Bayou, Mississippi.

In Riverside, California, the reason people standing in line at the bank were so upset when police came in and arrested two extortion suspects was that the reason they were standing in the line was to make an unauthorized withdrawal. The police, there in force with guns drawn, noticed the would-be bank robbers and arrested them, too. These lines at lunchtime are getting so long, Wells Fargo might have to set up a special line for bank robbers and extortionists.

Two Men Shoot
One Bullet

In Torrance, California, two young men charged in the shooting death of a drug dealer have been tried for murder. Because one of them talked to police and the other didn't, the judge allowed them to be tried before different juries. The prosecutor, Todd Rubenstein, told John Winkelman's jury that Winkelman fired the fatal shot, and he told Stephen Davis's jury that Davis fired the fatal shot. And both juries were convinced and found their respective defendants guilty. Winkelman and Davis both face possible life sentences now.

Defense attorneys are saying, "Wait a minute! How can the prosecutor tell one jury one thing and another jury another thing and get two convictions when there was only one bullet?" Prosecutor Rubenstein doesn't see any legal reason why he can't use the facts to make the case that one guy fired the bullet and then use the same facts to make the case that the other guy fired the bullet.

It was quite clear from the evidence, prosecutor Todd Rubenstein told John Winkelman's jury, that Winkelman fired the shot that killed drug dealer Willie Yen. He then told Stephen Davis's jury that Yen was shot from behind. And since Davis was the one who was behind Yen, it was clear from the evidence that he was the one who fired the fatal shot. Both juries believed Rubenstein, and Winkelman's jury found Winkelman guilty, and then an hour later, Davis's jury found Davis guilty.

Logic would suggest that if Davis fired the fatal shot, Winkelman didn't. And if Winkelman fired the fatal shot, then Davis didn't. The conclusions are mutually exclusive. But legally, says prosecutor Rubenstein, the separate juries heard the strongest case that he could make against each of the defendants. That's what his job is, Rubenstein says: to make the strongest case, each independent of the other.

Laurie Levenson, a law professor at Loyola Marymount University, who's also a former federal prosecutor, says from a legal point of view, you may be able to explain this. But from a commonsense point of view, it's not fair. Remember common sense? People used to talk about common sense all the time. But common sense is seldom invoked anymore. Seldom used either.

Bank Robbery 101

Anything worth doing is worth doing well, they say. You could argue that robbing a bank is never a good thing to do, it's a bad thing to do. It's always risky. But if you are going to do it, there are certain minimum standards of bank-robbing performance that have to be met if you're going to have any chance at all of achieving what, presumably, you had in mind. The would-be bank robber in Pierson, Florida, did not get caught, although it is still possible he could be; but he took a terrible chance and he didn't get any money at all because he missed at least one fundamental component of a bank robbery, and that is a bank. What he thought was a bank was the city water department. He didn't even get any water.

The right way to pull off a bank robbery, if I understand the bank robber movies correctly, is to plan everything with absolute precision. You've got to case the place methodically, find out where the cameras are exactly; exactly where the guards are going to be stationed, when they change duty; where the money is, precisely how and when it's brought in and out; and, of course, how and when to make your getaway.

This fellow who tried to rob a bank in Pierson, Florida, made some preparations. Apparently he did have a gun, and he did prepare his stickup note, and maybe he did case the place, I don't know. If so, maybe he saw that there weren't any bank cameras and there weren't any bank guards. That should have been his first clue that maybe it wasn't a bank. And there weren't any lines or ATM machines either, or many customers, for that matter. The people he thought were making deposits and withdrawals may have been in there writing out checks to pay their water bills, because, in fact, this was not a bank. It was the Pierson Water Department.

When he walked up to what he thought was a teller's window and showed his gun and stickup note, the city employee at the window told him she didn't have any money, and she opened the cash drawer to show him, and he just shrugged sheepishly and walked out of there.

If you're going to have a bank robbery, you really do have to have a bank. There is a bank in that same building, but this was not it, as the poor would-be bandito now surely realized. But he decided apparently to call a halt to his bank-robbing efforts for the day. It was April Fools' Day and he was the fool. Sounds to me as if this fellow was not cut out to be a bank robber. Maybe he should find another line of work altogether.

Catch No
Thieves

Within the space of two and a half hours one day recently, Wally Bergram, the manager of a 7-Eleven store in Odessa, Texas, was honored for being such a good manager and doing what he was supposed to do and was then fired for catching a thief, which he was not supposed to do. "This has sort of ruined the holidays for me," says Wally. He's out of a job now. Not that he wasn't a good manager. In fact, the same day he was fired, December 9, he had been honored at a luncheon thrown by his employers, Southwest Convenience Stores, Incorporated, for increasing sales in his store yet keeping overtime costs down. And then he was summoned to headquarters and dismissed because of what had happened on December 9.

That day, as he was walking out of his storeroom, he spotted three youths trying to steal some beer. One of the three attacked him, Bergram says. So Wally grabbed him, tied him up with a trash bag and held him until the police arrived. The other two guys ran off and escaped. Bergram says he was only acting in self-defense. "These punk kids," he says, "have no regard for anybody or anything. I didn't want anybody to get hurt."

Well, nobody did get hurt, as it turns out, except Wally. He was told he had violated a policy that forbids standing up to suspected criminal activity. "The penalty for confronting a criminal is termination," they told him. "There is no exception. You're fired." And no recourse, either. District manager Nick Papas says there are no gray areas. Store policy is it's better to lose a six-pack of beer now and then than to risk a gun battle or other violence where people could get killed.

Well, how about the good work as manager? Well, how about the 7-Eleven store's increased sales? How about the decreased overtime? How about the honor that they had given him? Well, all those things were good and they had duly honored him for it, but catching the thief—well, that was a bad thing, and he has been duly fired for that.

I'm sure the thieves out there are going to be fascinated to hear that the manager of any 7-Eleven store will be fired if he offers any resistance to them whatsoever. As for Bergram, he now knows that no good deed will go unpunished.

The Writer's
Cramp Punishment

Mike Erwin learned something about crime and punishment long before he became a judge in the Louisiana court system. When he was in high school many, many years ago, he committed the crime of talking out of turn in class. His punishment was to write out "I will not talk in class unless called upon" until he was blue in the face. That lesson wasn't forgotten. Now that Erwin's sitting on the bench, he sometimes metes out the same punishment.

JUDGE MIKE ERWIN: Well, I just think if you have to sit there and write "I will not steal other people's property" five thousand times that you're going to remember it.

That's why for the past three years he's been assigning home-
work to young adults who've been convicted of misde-
meanors in his Baton Rouge court.

JUDGE ERWIN: I had a guy who was accused of being a
Peeping Tom. I had him write several thousand times "I will
not peep in other people's windows." I had a lady who I
thought had done something that wasn't real smart, and I
made her write "I will not ever do stupid things again."

The idea behind this is simple enough: get people to focus on
their wrongdoing.

JUDGE ERWIN: Make them think about what they've done to
maybe realize the error of their ways, and, if nothing else, at
least to add some type of punishment other than just maybe
paying a fine.

Almost all the criminals go along with the sentence because
they think it beats the alternative, going to jail. And Judge
Erwin says it's effective too, because once someone has written several thousand times that they're not going to do something anymore, they tend not to do it anymore.

JUDGE ERWIN: None of the people who've been assigned to
write lines have come back that I can remember.

The worst part of the punishment may be the boredom and, of
course, the writer's cramp. But it's not unconstitutional, the
judge believes.

JUDGE ERWIN: I wouldn't think that in any way, shape or form it could be considered cruel and unusual punishment.

The judge does check the assignment once it's completed, but how can he be sure that each list is the work of one person? Could it be that some offenders are getting by with a little help from their friends?

JUDGE ERWIN: Think of how hard that would be for you to get your friends and relatives to help you do that. "You're crazy. I'm not going to write five hundred lines for you. Get out of here!"

A Lesson
Learned

Sometimes parents can teach a youngster a lesson by letting him take the consequences of his own misdeeds rather than letting him off the hook by taking care of the problem themselves.

The parents of eighteen-year-old Justin Ballenger of St. Johns, Arizona, decided not to pay a twelve-hundred-dollar fine Justin was levied for his conviction on charges of possession of marijuana. David and Marcia Ballenger thought it would teach Justin a lesson to pay it himself. But since they wouldn't pay the $1,200 and Justin didn't have $1,200, off he went to the Apache County jail for a week.

Justin served his time. While he was in there, he was allowed to use the telephone to make collect calls, and so he called home at least once every day; sometimes more than once, I think.

Like many jails, the Apache County jail has an arrangement with a private telephone company that charges much higher rates than the larger, well-known telephone companies. And when Papa Ballenger got his telephone bill later, he nearly went through the roof. Son Justin, who was in jail because his parents would not pay his twelve-hundred-dollar fine, had made $1,425 worth of collect telephone calls, including one twenty-two-minute call home that cost $125.

Zero Plus Dialing, a company in San Antonio, got the contract for the Apache jail phone service by paying the jail a hefty fee, as it does with more than a hundred other jails across the country. "It's ridiculous," says Marcia Ballenger. "I think it's a bigger crime than what Justin did. I'm not paying it," says David Ballenger. "Zero. They can take my phone out."

Prisoners have complained about being a captive audience for these little telephone companies that make deals with the jails. But so far the courts have not seen fit to interfere with the management of jails to the extent of telling them what phone companies they can or can't do business with.

The moral is that sometimes, when you try to teach your kid a lesson, you learn something yourself. And when you think you've saved $1,200, it can cost you $1,400.

Stone Walls Do
Not a Prison Make

Ivory White is thirty-five years old, serving a four-year prison sentence for the manufacture and distribution of drugs. Now, a man serving a four-year prison term is acutely aware of how much time he has left. So the other day, when the guards came and told him he was a free man and could go home now, Ivory told them no, they were making some mistake, he still had years to go. But the authorities paid no attention and insisted he was free to go, and go he did. It was a mistake, though. And it wasn't until several hours later that the police in Pontiac, Michigan, boarded a Chicago-bound bus and recaptured Ivory White.

Meanwhile, in Tacoma, Washington, community activist Willie Baker doesn't belong in jail. He's not a violent criminal or anything and the authorities have tried to get him to go home. They've left his cell door open. They've explained to him that all he needs to do is post a $125 bond. Somebody else, a supporter of his, put the money up. All he had to do was sign the bond and he wouldn't do it, so the supporter took the money back. He says he's not leaving until Tacoma apologizes. He's had a long-running feud with local authorities there in Tacoma. He's been critical, to say the least, about the way they run the Safe Streets neighborhood safety program. He's argued against the Hilltop Action Coalition, the Pierce County auditor at city council meetings until they wished he'd go home, almost as much as the sheriff wishes he'd go home now. Sheriff Mark French wanted to let him go on his own recognizance, but Baker wouldn't sign those papers, either.

And in Santa Ana, California, a man described as scruffy-looking gave a note to a bank teller demanding $2,000. He didn't take the money and run. He took the money and stayed. When police got there, they found him sitting on a couch in the bank, reading a newspaper, waiting for them. Apparently, he wanted to go to prison. Robbing a bank was his way of getting a roof over his head and three squares a day.

Apparently prisons aren't what they used to be. People on the outside trying to get in; people on the inside not wanting to leave.

Tools of Escape

Prisoners have been known to come up with some pretty fancy ideas about ways to escape, or try to. Just about any object that comes into their hands can be a potential tool to be used to attempt to escape. There's one story reported on the news wires recently about a convicted armed robber who's facing a six-year term in Parkhurst Prison on the Isle of Wight who plotted an escape by making ingenious use of a fluorescent-yellow felt pen. Think about it. If you were a prisoner trying to escape, can you think of some way that you might use a fluorescent-yellow felt-tip pen as an escape tool? A saw, maybe a blowtorch, pickax or row of twisted bed sheets, these I could see, but a felt-tip yellow pen?

A guard at Parkhurst Prison walked past a prison cell and then did a double take and took a closer look at what the convict inside was doing. This man was looking in the mirror and coloring his face bright yellow using a fluorescent-yellow felt-tip pen. When the authorities went inside to take a closer look, they saw that the man had painted his whole face yellow and his ears and his neck and his hands and his arms. They told him to strip, and sure enough, he had colored his legs and his feet yellow, too—his chest and his back and all of him—I mean, everything was this bright fluorescent yellow.

Now, you'd think offhand that this would make it more difficult for him to escape. "Hello. What's that fluorescent-yellow person over there doing?" The whole idea of escaping and milling into the crowd is based on the idea of not sticking out. A fluorescent-yellow person is bound to stick out.

Under questioning, the inmate broke down and confessed that his plan was to make the prison authorities think he had a nasty case of jaundice and they'd transfer him to someplace outside the prison from which place he could more easily escape.

On the Isle of Wight, a convict fellow,
Used a marker that was yellow
To make the guards and others present
Think that he had turned fluorescent
And get him to a doctor quick
Because, to them, he'd look so sick.
His yellow skin, from foot to face,

Looked like a real bad jaundice case.
At least, he hoped it would, they say,
So that from there, he'd get away.
But then they found him out one night.
So he's still on the Isle of Wight.

The Hair
Bargain

Back in the days of the wild, wild West, the sheriff used to put a price on the head of certain outlaws. Well, these days in Harris County, Texas, one innovative magistrate has put a price on the accused's scalp. Tony Polumbo lets young offenders who come into his court pay for their crimes with hair. Justice of the Peace Tony Polumbo sees seventy-five to a hundred youths a week in his court in Houston. Many of them are gang members, lots of them guilty of getting into fights. The law gives Polumbo plenty of latitude, and he needs it because today's kids have plenty of attitude.

TONY POLUMBO: You know, justice—the way they administered it in the past—just doesn't work.

That's why Polumbo started offering to buy kids' hair—not for cash. Youths exchange haircuts for a reduction in the number of community service hours they're sentenced to serve.

POLUMBO: If they have eighty hours to do, I will offer them ten to fifteen hours—whatever the market rate is at that particular time—for the unusual part of their hair.

OSGOOD: Unusual hair?

POLUMBO: A lot of them have short hair, and then at the bottom part of it, they let it grow real long. It could be real long hair. It could be hair that I've seen is shaved on the side with a strip long on the top. It's just different kind of hair.

The judge doesn't send kids to the barber to make a fashion statement. He says the hair is making a social statement.

POLUMBO: The strange way the hair is cut or combed is becoming the conformance of the subculture group.

A subculture, says Polumbo, that is encouraging kids not to take responsibility. He hopes making them look different will get them to think differently and maybe act differently. It's up to them.

POLUMBO: About 80 percent of them accept it. And nothing happens to them if they don't. It's just a business deal. But let me tell you something. They're pretty smart if they do, because guess what? They get fifteen hours off, and they can always let it grow back out.

For some of the kids, though, says Polumbo, the haircut can be just the beginning.

POLUMBO: Yeah, a lot of them started combing their hair neat, and they started feeling better about themselves. Because, see, I found out a long time ago, you and I and everybody in society act according to what we think of ourselves. I mean, it's just human nature. The more you think of yourself, the better you're going to act.

"Act" as in behave.

The Slammer

Sometimes if you're miffed about something, you leave the room in a huff. There is a temptation to punctuate your departure by slamming the door behind you. This can be extremely satisfying to the slammer and extremely irritating to the slammee. And although it is not considered good manners, it is not against the law most of the time. Nevertheless, for slamming the wrong door in the wrong place, Michael Wydler has spent the last couple of months in the slammer.

To slam the door as you leave a room provides a punctuation designed to insult the person you're walking out on and to get their hackles up. But there's nothing they can do about it ordinarily. However, the door that Michael Wydler of suburban Pittsburgh slammed behind him back in June happened to be the door to the courtroom of Allegheny County Judge Donald Mackin, who had just refused to waive filing fees for a divorce from Wydler's wife, Peggy. One gets the impression that there might have been a few slammed doors around the Wydler household over the months preceding the divorce filing.

Anyway, Wydler told the judge that he only made $10,034 during the previous ten months, and so he couldn't very well afford to pay the filing fee. And it was when the judge said that he had to pay it anyway that Wydler walked out of the courtroom and slammed the door behind him, whereupon the judge sentenced him to six months in jail for criminal contempt of court. Wydler was arrested later that day and sent to the Allegheny County jail. "What are you in for, Wydler?" "Well, they got me on a door-slamming rap."

Wydler's lawyers brought him back before the judge on August 5 and he apologized for his behavior, and he told the judge that he was getting counseling about managing his anger. But Judge Mackin said he still thought he detected a tone of disrespect and ordered him back to jail to finish his six-month sentence, and so back to jail he went.

But the American Civil Liberties Union stepped in on his behalf, lawyers arguing that this is something that should not happen in America. Judge Mackin's arrogant attitude toward a litigant appearing before him showed a lack of judicial restraint, the filing said. The lawyers filed an emergency petition. Later, the Pennsylvania Superior Court ordered Wydler released pending resolution of the case.

When you slam a door behind you, it feels good to hear the "bam!"
But you do have to be careful, though, whose door it is you slam.

A Patient's Right
to be Ignored

A man in Norfolk, Virginia, who sawed off his right hand because he thought it was possessed by the devil refused to let surgeons reattach it because he said he believed he would go to hell if they did. So they went to a judge, who ruled that if a man doesn't want to have his hand reattached, the hospital and doctors have no right to do so against his wishes, so they didn't. And now, guess what? The man is suing the hospital and the surgeon for $3.35 million for not doing it, saying they should have done it against his wishes.

A man has a right to change his mind, and thirty-two-year-old Thomas W. Passmore has now changed his mind about having his right hand reattached. It's a little too late now, of course, but doctors at Sentara Norfolk General Hospital might have been able to reattach the hand shortly after Passmore, who had been working on a construction job, sawed it off with a circular saw. But Passmore was adamant. If he wanted it on, he wouldn't have sawed it off in the first place, and the reason he did was that he thought he saw the numbers 666 on it and believed that to be a demonic sign, and the number of the beast is 666. He also remembered the biblical passage that goes, "If thy right hand offend thee, cut it off," and so he did. And he refused to give the hospital and the surgeon his permission to reattach it. So they contacted a judge, who told them that was right; they could not do it if Passmore didn't want them to.

Under Virginia state law, a doctor or a hospital cannot be held liable for withholding treatment if a judge approves that action and the patient is capable of an informed decision. Now Passmore's lawyers are saying that he was not capable of an informed decision. Why, nobody in his right mind would have done what he did, they say. And besides, he had told the doctors he had a history of psychiatric disorders, including manic depression, and that he had not slept or eaten much, and that thoughts had been racing through his mind for the week or so leading up to that day. And the doctors and the hospital never told the judge that the man was incompetent, and the judge, apparently, didn't realize from the facts of the case that a man who saws his hand off and doesn't want it reattached must be incompetent. Passmore's lawyers now say the hospital and doctors should have gone to his parents or his sister, anybody who would overrule what Passmore himself was saying at the time.

Since they didn't, the suit implies, it's their fault that Passmore doesn't have a right hand now, so they should pay him $3.35 million.

I suppose the hospital could always say the devil made them do it.

Bad Days

There are days when nothing seems to go right and we can't seem to get a break and everything we try to do turns out badly. Our tendency, on days like that, is to blame it on the day or blame it on somebody else. What we don't like to admit is that maybe we had something to do with it. When you're hot, you're hot, and when you're not, maybe you're doing something wrong.

Take Steve King in Decatur, Alabama, for example. Mr. King had an idea of getting some money by robbing a convenience store. Now, that is not a very good idea in the first place; it's certainly not a very original idea. But any chance of success with it was spoiled by the fact that when he ran out of the place, he left his car keys and his wallet behind, and in his wallet was his driver's license with his name and address on it. So he had to run back in to get the keys. He forgot about the wallet. Then his car broke down. And he went to his girlfriend's house at three in the morning where three other guys ganged up on him and beat him up. So he's now in jail on $10,000 bond. In any event, it was not his day, but it was his own fault.

There's a story on the wires about a man in Perth, Australia, who worked at a pet shop but was fired because his boss caught him stealing. Then while serving a short jail term for that offense, he came up with a scheme for getting back at the boss. He bought six ordinary green parrots, painted them with a reddish-brown hair dye so they would look like rare Indian ring-necked parrots, worth $5,500 each, and then arranged for a courier to swap his six painted birds with the pet shop for twenty-one authentic parrots worth $23,000. Anyway, a friend tipped off the police. So now the man, Denom Perez, is back in the cage himself.

And in Winfield, Kansas, two inmates serving time for burglary and theft broke out of the Cowley County jail and hired a limousine to drive them away. It was through the limo company that they were tracked to a hotel in Louisville, where they were arrested and a large sum of money was confiscated, police say.

If you're on the lam and you have a large sum of money, hiring a limo might seem like a good idea, but it's not.

VII.

Current
Affairs

The Style
Police

There are many ways kids express their individuality, their creativity, independence and defiance of the accepted modes of behavior and dress. And one is to dress exactly the same as all the other kids—certain kind of sneakers, certain kind of shirts and pants, all in certain colors and worn a certain way. Today a lot of kids wouldn't be caught dead wearing a baseball cap frontwards.

The causes of youth violence are many and complex and run deep in the structure of our society. But most of the steps that are taken to deal with the problem are simple. Maybe "simplistic" would be a better word—right on the surface, not very deep at all.

For example, at the Sunrise Mall in Corpus Christi, Texas,

one of the things they're doing about the crime situation is outlawing the wearing of baseball caps with the peak facing backwards. Some young people, and their parents, too, say that that's just the style. They don't see how turning baseball caps around with the peak facing front is going to affect the crime situation one way or the other.

But the Sunrise Mall security director, Scott Mandell, says, "I would rather have parents be upset at me than ask me why I let their kid be shot at the mall."

Last month at a mall in the Dallas suburb of Irving, a couple of kids were shot and wounded, and a passerby was killed. But there's no evidence at all that baseball caps frontwards or backwards had anything to do with it. Some law-enforcement people say they think baseball caps backwards are associated with gang affiliation.

Of course, baseball caps were made to be worn with the peak in the front to shade the eyes from the sun, but catchers, when they're behind the plate, have to wear them backwards because the face mask wouldn't fit otherwise. I can see why malls might be concerned if somebody were to come swaggering along wearing what's been called "the tools of ignorance": a backwards baseball cap, a face mask, shin guards and a chest protector. It might look as if he expected somebody to throw something at him.

We have a wonderful way of making controversy over the inconsequential so as not to have to deal with anything difficult. Now, instead of thinking about anything real when it comes to crime and youth violence, the controversy's about backwards baseball caps. When there's a serious problem, we'll do just about anything rather than face up to it frontwards.

Schools vs. Prisons

One way to tell what we think is important is to look at what we spend our money on. The more important it is, the more willing we are to pay—am I right? That's one of the reasons we spend a lot of money on health care. It's because we have excellent medical people and facilities here, and we are willing to pay for them—or have somebody pay for them anyway.

When a lot of premium American cars are sold here—and we do think cars are important—we say the auto manufacturers are doing a good job, and we try to encourage that. But when we spend a lot on premium health care because we think that's important, it's taken as a sign something's terribly wrong, and the government wants to discourage it by the re's—

reinventing, restructuring, redesigning, reengineering the whole kit and caboodle.

And speaking of what's important, it's obvious we Americans must think prisons are more important than schools. It seems everybody in government, from the president on down, is talking tough about crime now. "You do the crime, you do the time," "Three strikes and you're out"—all that sort of stuff. Actually, that should be three strikes and you're in—in prison and they throw away the key.

Talk about a growth industry. We can't build jails and prisons fast enough to hold our growing prison population, which has about tripled since 1980. At the end of that year, we had 315,974 people behind bars. Now our prison population is more than 925,000.

Talk about what we think is important. Did you realize that 70 percent of our prison space today has been built since 1985? It cost us $32 billion, but what the heck, it's worth it, right? It's important. By the way, only 11 percent of our classrooms were built in the eighties or nineties.

Here are some more stunning numbers: It costs about $5,600 a year, on the average, to keep a kid in a falling-apart public school, about $18,000 to keep a convict in a shiny new prison. We have to keep the prisons up because there's a constitutional mandate against cruel and unusual punishment. Nothing in there about overcrowded schools with leaky roofs, peeling paint, faulty wiring.

We're not able to keep all our school-aged kids in school, but we're not keeping all our criminals in prison either. Thirty-five million crimes are committed each year, but only 450,000 people go to jail. But which do we think are more important, the schools or the prisons? The prisons, apparently.

Save the
Children

The leading cause of death among American children from ten to nineteen years old is accidents—car accidents, mostly. The second leading cause of death in that age group is— what would you guess: cancer, heart disease, drugs, AIDS? Those things are on the list, but farther down. No, the second leading cause of death for American kids is gunfire, mostly not accidental. Of the 5,751 childhood gun deaths in this country in 1993—the last year for which we have numbers—3,661 were gun murders. Another 1,460 were gun suicides. Is there anything we Americans can do to stop kids from blowing each other's brains out? Yes, there is, but it involves using our own brains.

It's the government's duty and responsibility to protect our own citizens. That's why there are no American children at the U.S. Mission in Liberia right now. They were removed to get them out of the way of the shooting in Liberia's civil war. This we can do. But it seems we have not been able to find a way to get our own children out of the way of the shooting right here in our own country.

Since 1979, more American children have died from gunfire than members of the U.S. military killed in the Vietnam War and every war or military action we've been in since. In the Bush administration, Congress passed a law making it illegal to have a gun within a thousand feet of a school, but then the Supreme Court struck that law down, saying the activity being regulated was outside federal jurisdiction. There's an effort in Congress to lift gun restrictions, including the 1994 ban on assault weapons.

Maybe we should consider sending our children away for a while, as Londoners did with their children during the blitz in World War II. We have our own home-grown blitz of gunfire right now. Perhaps, if we put our minds to it, we can figure out some way to stop it.

"True Facts"

Do you know the difference between a fact and a true fact?
Well, let me explain. A fact is simply something that is or
was. A "true fact" is more important than a plain old run-
of-the-mill fact. A true fact is one that supports your own
opinions.

Obviously, a fact that bolsters your own case is a much truer
fact than the one that indicates the other guy is right. Those
are the ones he thinks are true facts, but he's wrong, of course.
There's never been a better example of the true facts dilemma
than the efforts in recent years to come up with objective
standards for teaching our kids history—world history and
American history. What to put in, what to leave out; what to

say and what not to say. It all depends on what you're trying to prove.

They have come out with yet another revision of the proposed national standards for teaching history in America's secondary schools. This time they don't neglect George Washington or ignore James Madison, Thomas Edison and Benjamin Franklin; and they don't accentuate the negative—the Depression, the Ku Klux Klan, McCarthyism, racism and so on—quite as much as the first proposed standards did a couple of years ago. And there's more in there now about the achievements of women and minorities and about science. And this time it doesn't read as the first standards did, like a handout from the Democratic National Committee, idealizing Democrats like Roosevelt, Kennedy and Johnson, demonizing Republicans like Coolidge and Hoover, blaming them for the stock market crash of '29 and the Great Depression.

Some bipartisan review committees like this version much better, but some critics are still critical, and some aren't so sure that national history teaching standards are a very good idea in the first place. Conservative groups do not like some of the things the teachers here and there across the United States have been telling our kids about their country. But they worry even more about voluntary national standards being picked up by state and local education authorities, thus creating what Robert Morrison of the Family Research Council calls "deadening conformity."

History is "his" story and "her" story and yours and mine, and all of us believe in reporting the facts. However, some facts, the ones at variance with our own notion of the "true facts," only confuse the issue, and should be omitted.

A fact is true by definition,
Which puts us in a strange position.
We only see what we're supposed to
And cannot face what we're opposed to.
The truth is in how one reacts
To unadulterated facts.
Although no fact can be untrue,
I disagree with quite a few.
My facts are better than my brother's.
Some facts are truer than some others.

When Is a Hate Crime
Not a Hate Crime?

A nineteen-year-old in Illinois who pleaded guilty last month to helping his brother and a friend build a cross, wrap it in a sheet and set fire to it on a family's lawn was convicted of a hate crime and sentenced to three years in prison. But no sooner did he start serving his prison term than he was set free and his conviction was nullified because the family on whose lawn he and his accomplices had burned a cross was a white family. The judge ruled that it would only have been a hate crime if the victims had been black. How about that?

The reason nineteen-year-old Damon Nantz and his brother and a friend burned a cross on the lawn of a white couple there in Pekin, Illinois, was that the woman in the house, Carla Kant, has a sixteen-year-old daughter who lives with her father in

Peoria, and she would visit sometimes with her boyfriend, who happens to be an African-American.

But shortly after Nantz was convicted and started serving his three-year prison term, his attorney found out that in another case where some minors had been accused of displaying pictures of violent acts toward blacks to a person who was white, the Fifth District Illinois Court of Appeals had ruled that since the victim was white, it could not have been a hate crime under the state law.

The law says a hate crime is an assault or some similar crime inspired by race, religion, gender or several other specific attributes. It doesn't say specifically that the victim has to be black, but the court ruled that that's what the legislature must have had in mind, and the boys were released.

It didn't matter that the pictures were full of racism, hate and bigotry. What mattered was that the person they showed the pictures to was white. And based on the precedent, Circuit Court Judge Scott Shore has ordered the release of Damon Nantz and dismissed all charges against the others who were involved in the cross burning in question, since the homeowners on whose lawn the cross was burned are white.

Apparently, if the Illinois state legislature has anything against burning crosses on white people's lawns, it is going to have to rewrite the legislation to make that fact clear to the judges of that state.

Niggardly

When David Howard, an aide to Washington, D.C.'s Mayor Anthony Williams, was describing how he administered a government fund, he used the word "niggardly"—which has absolutely nothing to do, etymologically or any other way, with the N word . . . the racial slur. "Niggardly" means miserly. Its origin is Scandinavian. But some people who didn't know this were offended nevertheless—and even some who did know better said it was bad judgment for Howard to have used a word that sounds anything like, or could possibly be mistaken for, the N word. Howard is white, incidentally. Anyway, there were calls for his resignation and he resigned, and Mayor Williams *accepted* the resignation. Although Williams has since said that he might offer Howard another job doing something else "if he is ultimately judged to have done nothing wrong."

So it is that the language is held hostage to ignorance in the guise of political correctness. Perfectly good words can become unusable because of misunderstanding. Howard was one of Mayor Williams's aides. The word "aides" now is compromised. Mr. Howard happens to be gay. The word "gay," unless meaning homosexual, has fallen out of use. It was very different back when our hearts were young and gay, when donning our gay apparel meant something else entirely. I once quoted an honorable businessman as saying his company "would never cheat or deceive or welsh." Some Welsh people took exception to that, and rightly so, as it turns out. I had never realized that the verb to welsh had anything to do with Welshmen, or - women. You can't say "Indian giver" anymore, of course—in fact you can't say "Indian" unless you're talking about somebody from New Delhi or Calcutta. It's not what such words mean that can bring trouble down on you, but rather what somebody else might somehow *think* they do.

A few weeks later, Mayor Williams rehired David Howard. "I acted too hastily," he said. "While it is necessary for a mayor to act decisively, it is not always necessary to act hastily."

Seems to me there was nothing necessary in this whole incident.

The Swarthmore
Solution

Persistence is supposed to be a virtue. If at first you don't succeed, try, try again. But if at first a guy doesn't succeed in getting a date with a girl he wants to go out with, if he does try, try again, he can get in trouble. If you don't buzz off when somebody tells you to buzz off, the authorities may be on your case.

At Swarthmore College, an exclusive liberal arts college in Philadelphia, a freshman named Ewart Yearwood tried to get a date with Alexis Kleinensmith and did not succeed. And so he tried and tried again. And now, the administration has offered to pay him tuition money, transportation and book costs to go to school somewhere else.

Ewart Yearwood is eighteen years old. Last semester, this

Swarthmore College freshman shaved his head, revealing some scars on his scalp. And he admits that he looks mean when he's not smiling. But he hoped, nevertheless, to charm his classmate Alexis Kleinensmith. He couldn't keep her out of his mind. She couldn't keep him out of her hair. He'd ask her out, seek her out on campus, call her at night—nothing worked. Alexis was not charmed. She was, in fact, put off.

She complained to the Swarthmore administration and to the police and to the Delaware County District Attorney's Office that Ewart Yearwood was sexually harassing her. Yearwood agreed to stay at least forty feet away from Alexis. But a disciplinary committee decided he violated that agreement and suspended him for the spring semester.

Ewart appealed to President Albert H. Bloom, assuring him that if he was suspended, he would sue Swarthmore. Lawyer Harvey Solarglade said the case resulted from "an outrageous infestation of political correctness."

Well, President Bloom looked into this, discussed it with Ewart and decided it was not a case of sexual harassment. However, he said, it was a case of intimidation, and intimidation was something up with which Swarthmore would not put either. So he didn't kick Ewart out exactly, but he did offer to pay the tuition, transportation, board and other expenses for him if he would be so kind as to go to college someplace else. Maybe they would let him back in next year, if he had counseling to deal with his problem, which Swarthmore would also pay for.

Ewart says, "They feel that I probably inadvertently, subconsciously release intimidating vibes and that I need counseling to better understand what it is in my behavior that makes people feel that way and how to be perceived as less intimidating."

Anyway, Ewart plans to register today at Columbia University in New York City.

Presumably, at Columbia they know how to deal with this sort of thing.

Negative
Campaigning

Polls indicate that many potential voters across the country have had it up to here with negative campaign ads. They think the spots are an insult to their intelligence. They say they resent them. They say they thoroughly dislike them and that they're completely turned off by them. Gee, I wonder why they say that.

Okay, here's how you write a negative campaign ad. Let's say you want to write one for candidate X, who's running against candidate Y. First you go to the thesaurus, not to look up synonyms for saint or hero to describe Mr. X, but rather, synonyms for villain to describe Mr. Y. And then you try to work in as many of these in the allotted thirty seconds as you possibly can.

"Here is contemptible candidate Y" is the opening thing that you
say.
Who is selfish and mean and ambitious, will let no one stand in
his way.
A no-good, unscrupulous, thoughtless and greedy, unprincipled
person is Y.
He hates widows and children and puppies and kittens because
he's that sort of a guy.
Candidate Y has a wandering eye and a preoccupation with sex.
This announcement prepared and paid for by Citizens for
Candidate X.

If it's X that you're trying to help Y defeat, you forget about Y
from the start,
And say, "Candidate X is incarnate excess, who'd be dangerous
if he was smart."
You'd suggest X is such a despicable lout that he hasn't stopped
beating his wife,
That he never did any constructive or decent or unselfish thing in
his life.

Some voters are saying they're not at all pleased by the negative
feeling of it.
It's the Tyson or Alomar school of debate with a mixture of
venom and spit.
Some will tell you that sportsmanship's not what it was, that it's
lost something noble and true.
And some people may say that in much the same way, our
democracy's lost something, too.

The Ecuadoran
Transition Process:
February 1997

We hardly ever hear anything about Ecuador in the news. It's not been exactly in the world spotlight. But it's impossible to ignore what's happening there now. After a wild six months as president, Abdalá Bucaram, the singing, dancing politician whose governing style has been eccentric to say the least, was voted out of office by Ecuador's congress on the grounds of mental incapacity.

Bucaram, who often cheerfully refers to himself as El Loco, called it a congressional coup and refused to step down. The Ecuadoran military, while promising not to stage a military coup, huddled all night with Bucaram trying to find a way out of the crisis. Under Ecuadoran law, there is no long, drawn-out impeachment process for dumping a president. All it takes is forty-two votes out of the eighty-two legislators in the congress. And after a long and contentious debate overnight, the congress voted President Abdalá Bucaram out of office, saying in effect that the man who has been calling himself El Loco is, indeed, loco.

Bucaram took office in August after a campaign that included a road show in which he joked and danced and belted out his own rendition of "Jailhouse Rock" in Spanish, promoting his CD recording of the same. The voters found it entertaining enough to elect him president. One of the first things he did in office was to invite Lorena Bobbitt to lunch at the national palace. She's the Ecuadoran woman famous for cutting off her American husband's penis.

As amused as some Ecuadorans may have been by El Loco, they were not amused by the government's austerity measures that have tripled rates for electricity and telephone service. There have been almost daily protest demonstrations since January and the nationwide strike the other day. Students, farmers, Indians, labor organizations and others took to the streets in cities and towns across Ecuador shouting, "¡Olé! ¡Olé! ¡Olé! Thief! Thief! Thief! Go away! Go away!"

Bucaram fired four of his cabinet members, including his own brother Adolfo Bucaram, who was the social welfare minister. In declaring Bucaram mentally unfit to be president, Congress named its own leader, Fabian Alarcon, as interim president, but Vice President Rosalia Arteaga, who had broken with Bucaram, says she should be the one to take over.

Meanwhile, Bucaram is barricaded in the presidential palace, refusing to yield. No, the situation there in Ecuador is not what one would call stable. But it's not dull there, I can tell you that.

Job Opening

There's a great job opening out there for the right person. The job pays well. There's opportunity for rapid advancement. And you would have the satisfaction of doing something that would benefit your country as well as yourself. The key to the benefit program, however, is staying alive. Because your country—the country that you would be doing something for—is Iraq. You have to be an Iraqi. Sorry, this is not an equal opportunity opening. Non-Iraqis need not apply. And the reason the job pays so well is that it is considered highly dangerous work. But there's $91 million waiting for the right Iraqi to come along and lead the opposition to Saddam Hussein.

One of the ways in which the United States is different from Iraq is that you would never see an impeachment inquiry in

Baghdad, with Iraqi politicians and lawyers looking into Saddam Hussein. Questioning his ethics, his veracity, his fitness to be president of Iraq. There is nobody in that country you could describe as the Kenneth Starr of Iraq. The life expectancy of such a person over there would be extremely short.

And there are no polls there like the ones we have, reporting that Saddam Hussein's approval rating has gone up or down three points. There, if somebody calls you up and asks you if you approve of the way Saddam Hussein is handling his job, you have to be really careful about the answer you give. If an Iraqi is critical of Saddam, or is willing to identify him- or herself as being opposed to this man who has wielded power there for thirty years, you can be sure that this person is in London or Paris or someplace other than Baghdad, some country other than Iraq.

Saddam has executed members of his own family for looking at him cross-eyed. These days there are certain kinds of jobs that nobody wants to do anymore. Have you noticed that? This is one of them, I guess.

Nobody said it would be easy. But there's plenty of money, power, prestige and a place in history waiting for somebody. All we're asking him to do is one little thing. All he has to do is overthrow Saddam Hussein.

In Harm's Way

The cost of natural disasters in both money and human life is rising. The main reason is not that the earthquakes, storms, floods and forest fires are bigger or stronger than before, or that the dollar cost is more because of inflation.

Disaster costs are doubling or tripling every ten years because there are more of us living in places that are disaster-prone. In a special session of the American Geophysical Union, climatologists, geologists and other scientists discussed the reasons for this.

In the first eleven months of 1998, the world's economy suffered $89 billion in losses from natural disasters. Thirty-two thousand people were killed. Three hundred thousand lost their homes. El Niño had something to do with that, and La Niña after that. And although we're getting better at assessing the risks in a given area, more and more people are putting themselves in harm's way. We build our houses on fault lines and along the coast, and in floodplains where again and again the waters rise.

William Hooke of the U.S. Department of Commerce says people here are only beginning to seriously consider what might happen if a severe storm, drought, fire or other catastrophe should strike. They're beginning to realize, "Hey, if my house is flooded, maybe I'm being dumb for living where I do." We like views. We like living in those places where nature can be most destructive.

And we never seem to learn. What happened in Galveston in 1900 happened in Central America with hurricane Mitch almost a century later. Ten thousand dead as a result. The researchers say the patterns of disaster should give us some clue as to where not to build our homes.

But as Earth's population grows, more and more of us are living in the most vulnerable places and have become more and more dependent on technology, which is itself vulnerable.

Natural disasters will happen. "Acts of God" we call them. But the cost in lives and money demonstrates not the wrath of God, but the folly of man.

The Enemy

It's been said that human nature requires enemies. We have to have somebody to be against, to blame things on. When a war comes to an end, even a Cold War, it creates all sorts of problems for those concerned. If our old enemy, the Soviet Union, doesn't exist anymore, then who is the enemy? Surely there's got to be one. If godless communism is not the philosophy that's threatening us, then what *is* the philosophy that's threatening us? How can we stand for something unless we stand against something else?

"We have seen the enemy, and he is us," according to Walt Kelly's most famous Pogo utterance. We wouldn't have wars if we didn't have enemies. And we wouldn't have enemies if we weren't pretty sure somebody else was trying to do us in.

But it turns out once the war is over, we and our enemies often find that we have very much in common. And historians tell us if we hadn't made this tactical or diplomatic mistake, if we'd only done this or hadn't done that, the war could have been avoided altogether. Well, hindsight is 20/20, of course, but it can certainly be argued that past wars could have been avoided if only the people running the world had been smart enough to do the right thing.

War is not the only kind of man-made disaster or catastrophe on this planet, but it is one of the most destructive things, potentially the most destructive thing, we can do to each other, which is to say, to ourselves.

But we don't really need to make enemies of one another. Don't we have enemies enough? Common enemies in the earthquakes and windstorms and droughts and floods and famine and plagues that afflict us? Of course we do. We can't blame earthquakes and tornadoes on anybody. All we can do is try to learn more about them so that we can understand them and better cope with them.

We can blame government agencies for not preparing or reacting well enough, I suppose, but that's just our old blaming habit. The only enemies worth listing and fighting and going to war with are the common enemies that just possibly we could do something about if we pitched in and worked with each other instead of against. It should be all of us against disease, poverty, ignorance and the suffering that grows out of those things.

If we have met the enemy and he is us, it's time we called a truce, shook hands and made peace with ourselves.

VIII.

Money Draws Flies

Freeloading
Un-Americans

Many of us, maybe because of the way we were brought up, imagine that the people we owe money to—credit card companies, let's say—will think well of us and will be just as pleased as punch when we pay them the money we owe them. I always imagine the folks at Visa or MasterCard opening up the envelope at the end of the month, looking at my check and saying to themselves, "Good old Osgood, paid his bill in full again this month. What a splendid fellow he is!" . . . or words to that effect.

Aha! Well, was I ever wrong about that! The fact is that the credit card companies do not like it when you pay what they call "the full amount." What they really want you to pay is what they call "the minimum amount."

And the reason is that when you do that, you are, in effect, borrowing the balance at interest rates that are so high that once upon a time, not so long ago, a lender who charged that much would be sent to jail for violating the usury laws. So credit card companies hate it when you pay off your balance every month, and some of them may start charging you for it.

About 20 percent of the holders of GE Capital Corporation's GE Rewards MasterCard never have to pay any interest charges because whenever they get a bill, they pay the whole thing. The company informed these people recently that if they don't start carrying a balance, which is to say owing the company money, the company is going to start charging them $25 a year, even if they never use the card at all to buy anything. GE seems to feel that since there has been no annual fee for membership, its customers owe it to the company to owe them money.

Robert McKinley, the president of Ram Research, a credit card research company based in Frederick, Virginia, says, "The big thing now is: How do you extract income from the group of people who basically freeload onto the system?" How do you like that? Now you're a freeloader if you pay all your bills. "I think it's inevitable," says McKinley, "that you're going to see a penalty fee arise for those customers who do not incur interest charges."

My fellow freeloaders, do you not realize that by paying your credit bills on time and in full, you are taking bread from the tables of the families of the moneylenders? How could you have been so selfish, so thoughtless, so un-American?

How the Company
Could Con Edison

Some people don't like to gamble because they know the odds are against them. The odds always favor the house, but that doesn't mean that some gamblers don't get lucky sometimes. People do beat the odds, and there are circumstances, even when the odds do favor the house, that make it prudent to play anyway.

But here I'm not referring to gambling casinos; I'm referring to the insurance business. When you buy life insurance, for example, you are betting you're going to die. That is a sure bet, by the way. You will. The only question is when.

The way you beat the house—the insurance company, in this case—is to die sooner than they figured you would. By dying soon, you win. By living to a ripe old age, you lose. Losing is better than winning when it comes to life insurance.

So insurance is a bit of a crapshoot, but it's one in which you hope you lose, since if you win, it means the bad thing you were insuring yourself against happened. You had a car crash or some other kind of accident or a fire or you got sick or you died. That's the only way you can collect. Living to a ripe old age means you lose.

Which brings us to the case of Thomas Alva Edison.

The other day in West Orange, New Jersey, the Mutual Life Insurance Company of New York gave the Edison National Historic Site some policies that it had sold to Thomas Alva Edison as far back as 1893. He bought a $10,000 policy that year, after being turned down for life insurance by four other companies.

They turned him down for a lot of reasons. He was over-weight. He was five-foot-nine and change and weighed 186 pounds. And they turned him down because of his various conditions, as they used to call them in those days. Edison had chronic indigestion. He had a diabetic condition, a sinus condition, an ear condition, and he lived dangerously—hardly ever got a night's sleep. He slept in fits and starts.

The only reason Mutual was willing to sell him a policy at all is that he agreed to an exclusion. The company would not have to pay a death benefit if he was electrocuted. The company representative, Thomas Lanihan, who presented the policies to the historic site on Friday, quoted the policy as saying, in effect, "This guy fools around with something called electricity."

The actuaries at the time figured Tom Edison would live to be forty-two. He died in 1931 at the age of eighty-four. So there you go, the house won again.

Winning
and Losing

They say be careful what you pray for, because you may get it. When Buddy Post of Oil City, Pennsylvania, a former carnival worker and cook, bought his Pennsylvania Lottery ticket, he hoped and prayed, like everybody else who buys tickets, that he'd win. And he did. He won $16.2 million, and now he wishes he hadn't.

"Money draws flies," says Buddy Post. He won $16.2 million in the Pennsylvania State Lottery back in 1988, and since then he's been convicted of assault, his sixth wife left him, his brother was convicted of trying to kill him and his landlady successfully sued him for a third of the jackpot.

He bought a crumbling mansion with his winnings, but now

it's half filled with paperwork from bankruptcy proceedings and lawsuits. The gas has been shut off. "Money didn't change me," says Post. "It changed people around me that I thought cared a little bit about me, but only cared about the money." Now fifty-eight years old, he plans to sell off his seventeen future payments, face value nearly $5 million, for less than half that. The Pennsylvania Lottery may block the auction because it says winners can't sell future payments, but his bankruptcy lawyer says the auction is legal because it's being done in federal bankruptcy court, which supersedes the state courts.

Here are some of the things that have happened to Buddy Post. In 1992, he was ordered to give a third of his winnings to his former landlady, Ann Carpic, who claims she shared the ticket with him. During that dispute, he didn't have access to the lottery payments so he couldn't keep up with the legal fees and the bills for the bar, the used-car lot and the other failed business ventures that he started with relatives after winning the jackpot. His six-month-to-two-year jail sentence for assault is under appeal. Post says he simply fired a gun into the garage ceiling to scare off his stepdaughter's boyfriend, who was arguing with him about money. His brother, Jeffrey, was convicted of plotting to kill Buddy and his wife, Constance, in 1993 as part of a scheme to gain access to the lottery money.

When Post filed for bankruptcy in 1994, he was given a monthly allowance of $2,000. Constance, who had left him by then, gets $40,000 a year in support payments. Post now has about a half million dollars in debts, not counting taxes and legal fees. He hopes the proceeds of the auction will let him pursue the lawsuits that he's filed against police, judges and lawyers who he says conspired to take his money. He has also sold the rights to his life story to a movie company which he says wants the role of Buddy Post to be played by Jack Lemmon.

There's no word yet from Jack Lemmon.

Location,
Location,
Location

When you're hot, you're hot. And when you're not, well, you're not. Sol Hurok, the late, great concert impresario who knew every promotional and marketing trick in the book, used to say that if people don't want to come to see an attraction, nothing you can do will keep them from not coming. That's the way it is with the land in Lefors, Texas, apparently. They can't give it away.

Lefors is a sleepy little town seventy miles east of Amarillo. It has a lot of trees. That's unusual in the Texas panhandle, and the shade in the summertime may be the best thing about Lefors. It doesn't have too much else going for it, not since the oil bust of the 1980s and the tornado twenty years ago. Only two of the streets of Lefors are paved. Most of the six hundred people who live there commute to work at the prison or the chemical plant, both of which are in Pampa, a dozen miles away.

In an effort to boost their tax base and school population, the town fathers of Lefors offered a land giveaway, hoping to attract people to move there. All the winners had to do to get the land was agree to build a house or to move a mobile home onto the land within six months. They had a lot of entries, but the deadline for claiming your lot came and went, and only one person has expressed any interest in actually moving there.

The interested party is Vera Rodriguez. She is seventy years old, a retiree, living now in Bakersfield, California. She's never been to Texas, not even to check out her 50-by-125-foot parcel of land. And she's having some second thoughts. "I was hoping that this place was in the country," says Ms. Rodriguez. "I understand that it is a city. And I hear that you have winds galore. But they tell me that we can have a vegetable garden and plant fruit trees. I don't want to have cattle," she says, "but I would like to have chickens."

The Lefors city secretary, Virginia Maple, says she is real disappointed in the results of the land giveaway. "I would have thought that the winners would be eager to relocate here," she says. But former city councilman J. C. "Curly" Calloway says that he is not surprised at all. "We just don't have anything to draw people," he says.

Sol Hurok could have warned them "If people don't want to come, nothing you can do will keep them from not coming."

Atlantic City ATM
Machine Pays Off

In Atlantic City, as in Las Vegas, Reno and other gambling meccas, there are machines that pay you cash. Ordinarily, you have to put some money in first. More often than not, by the time you walk away from one of these slot machines, or one-armed bandits, as they're sometimes called, you have given it more money than it has given you—a lot more, in some cases.

But recently, for several hours there in Atlantic City, there was a machine that was paying out cash—a whole lot of cash—and not taking in any money at all. This was at a casino, the Grand, but it was not a slot machine; it was an ATM cash machine that ran amok, giving out hundred-dollar bills instead of twenty-dollar bills. And it took several hours on Thursday night and Friday morning before the management caught on.

Needless to say, this machine was quite popular for a while there.

By the time the security people from the Grand got to the PNC cash machine that was spending money like a drunken sailor and shut it down, the machine had already spewed out about $85,000 more cash than it was supposed to. Instead of dispensing twenties, it was hundred-dollar bills it was dishing out—five times the expected amount. Word spread pretty quickly, and among those lined up to take advantage of the overgenerous ATM machine were several casino employees who had heard about it.

How it happened that the machine was out of whack, or how many people walked away with more than they bargained for, we don't know, but the bad news for them is that before they could take out any money, they had to sign on, and having signed on, the machine has a record of who they are and who got how much. A spokesman for the New Jersey State Gaming Commission, whose name sounds, by the way, as if he was born on a racetrack, Keith Furlong, said that the individuals concerned will have to give the money back. In Atlantic City.

It's a wonderful feeling, as we know,
To win money when in a casino.
But an ATM jackpot does seem a bit crackpot.
They won't even do that in Reno.

The Price
of Farce

John Leonard—not my colleague John Leonard, the critic and *Sunday Morning* commentator, but a twenty-one-year-old business student by the name of John Leonard of Lynnwood, Washington—is suing PepsiCo, the company that makes Pepsi-Cola, because he claims he collected enough Pepsi points to win the $70 million Harrier jet fighter shown in the Pepsi Stuff TV commercials and that now Pepsi won't give him one. They say they were only kidding and they're suing him, trying to have his claims declared frivolous and asking for reimbursement for their legal fees. Leonard maintains that his lawsuit against Pepsi-Cola, demanding that the company give him a $70 million Harrier jet fighter plane, is not an attempt to get Pepsi to settle out of court. He says he and his friends saw the plane as an entrepreneurial venture and that maybe they'd be able to take customers for thrill rides. In any event, he says, "I am simply trying to take Pepsi up on an offer it made to the public." The offer he's talking about is the TV commercial for a Pepsi Stuff promotion in which customers who rack up points by drinking Pepsi beverages can claim a variety of prizes. And as a joke, this commercial winds up with a special deal for seven million Pepsi points, and that is the Harrier jet.

Leonard calls the company, finds out that he can buy Pepsi points for 10 cents apiece, and then rounds up five investors who commit to putting up the $700,000 that that would take. That would be a pretty good deal: a $70 million airplane for only $700,000. And he sent Pepsi 15 original Pepsi points and a check for $700,008.50 to cover the remaining 6,999,985 points, plus shipping and handling, the lawsuit says. And goes on to say, surprisingly, that on May 7, 1996, Pepsi failed and refused to process the items and, more important, failed and refused to provide the new Harrier jet. The company filed a preemptive suit against Leonard last month, asking to have his claim declared frivolous and to reimburse the company for its legal fees. Says Pepsi spokesman John Harris, "If we have to put disclaimers on spots that are obviously farces, where does it all end?" Where, indeed?

Be Prepared

If you're going to go into a retail business, you have to ask yourself, "What do the people in this area need?" Well, recently, as happens every so often in southern California, there was a reminder of what people need. Earthquake Outlet in Albany, California, sells just about everything you would need to prepare for the big one still to come.

FRANK WONG: They know they live in earthquake country, and it's like an insurance policy. You know, you just have to get it.

Frank Wong's store, just north of Berkeley, offers everything necessary to deal with natural disasters, quakes, fires, mud slides, snowstorms, whatever. Although, of course, the big demand now is for earthquake preparedness kits.

WONG: Fourteen different kinds from the inexpensive ten-dollar one to the $750 unit for fifteen people.

Wong says a basic kit for a family of four costs about $125.

WONG: You would have food, water, blankets, light sticks, flashlight, batteries, radio, first aid kit. You'd have rain ponchos, a whistle, Swiss Army–type knives, sanitary bags—a few things like that.

But to be really prepared, you should also have search-and-rescue tools, if only because you may have to save yourself.

WONG: Crowbars, goggles, gloves, hard hats—just to get out of the building you're in—sometimes if you're trapped.

Wong also sells a film for windows that keeps glass from shattering. He stocks fasteners you'd use to prevent household objects from flying through the air.

WONG: Industrial Velcro, cabinet fasteners to prevent the non-structural items like TV, faxes, refrigerators, microwave ovens from coming and smacking you in the face.

The store opened in 1989, but it was only after the most recent trembler that the crowds really started pouring in.

WONG: Prior to the earthquake we were doing, you know, $300 a day on average. After the earthquake, we're doing $10,000 a day.

Wong doesn't know how long it will last, but for now, he's packing them in the Earthquake Outlet.

WONG: What they're saying is that, "Gee, you know, I promised my loved one I'd do it. I'm finally doing it." And there's people also saying, "It's very wise to get prepared. I've been thinking about it for two years. I've got a note on my refrigerator, 'Do it.' I'm doing it now."

Guenther

L ike any individual who would stand to inherit an $80 mil-
lion fortune, Guenther lives very well. He lives on a luxu-
rious estate near Pisa, Italy, home of the famous Leaning Tower.
He has a maid. He has a chauffeur who takes him out for out-
ings in a limo. He has somebody run his Jacuzzi bath for him,
prepare his meals. He even has someone brush his teeth for him.

Unlike most of the very rich, however, Guenther IV is a dog.
He is the only son and heir of the late Guenther III, who inher-
ited $80 million from an eccentric German countess named
Carlotta Lievenstein, who died in 1991.

Responsible for Guenther IV is a lawyer in Pisa named
Antonella Signorini, who's trying to carry out the contessa's
wishes but has run into a little legal difficulty. The contessa

divided her time between her estate in the German town of Rosenheim and her estate in Faglia, near Pisa.

Unfortunately, the money is still in Germany, and some people there have contested the will. And so Guenther has not actually collected any of the money yet. But he is living at Faglia, at the estate, in what I think can be fairly called the lap of luxury, along with a pharmacist named Maurizio Mian, who was a dear friend of the contessa. "Why shouldn't a dog's teeth be brushed?" asks Mian. "Why shouldn't a dog have a Jacuzzi?"

Guenther's backers have, in his name, tried unsuccessfully to take over the Bologna football club and the Florence water polo team. And he's become a sponsor and honorary member of the Livorno water sports team, posing with them for pictures and all that.

This, according to Signorini, is in accordance with the wishes of the late contessa. "The contessa was crazy about animals," says Signorini. "She believed in their power and purity. She used to say 'Guenther is a symbol of power and honesty in a country where men are no longer honest.' "

Living near that Leaning Tower
Is a dog who symbolizes power.
Guenther proves a theory which
Says life is better when you're rich.

Your Tax Dollars
at Work:
Rat Department

Do you think of the government as your friend or as your enemy? Well, if you happen to be a rat living in Florida, it would all depend. It would depend on what kind of a rat you are, for one thing, and on which government agency you're talking about, because right now there are some government people trying to kill rats and others trying to save them.

Sometimes government agencies work at cross-purposes. The surgeon general's office, for example, is doing all it can to stop people from smoking, while the Department of Agriculture is doing all it can to help farmers grow tobacco. The taxpayers, of course, pay for both efforts.

Meanwhile, in Florida, the Centers for Disease Control has confirmed that a man in the Rudlands area, southwest of

Miami, has died of a rat-carried virus called hantavirus, and federal and local experts have scattered hundreds of aluminum rat traps baited with peanut butter. I always thought cheese was the traditional rat trap bait, but maybe it's mousetraps I was thinking of. Anyway, peanut butter is the best rat bait in the world, according to Dr. Gregory Gori, an epidemiologist who works for the CDC.

The government's rat patrol wants to trap and dissect enough rats to find out how widely the hantavirus has spread with the growth of the rat population in Florida following Hurricane Andrew in 1992. The crumbled buildings from the storm gave rats a place to breed. Health officials are going to ask FEMA, the Federal Emergency Management Agency, for $3.1 million to fund an anti-rat campaign.

Meanwhile, the U.S. Fish and Wildlife Department says its save-the-rat campaign is going very well, thank you. So well that they may take the Key Largo wood rat off the endangered species list. The government has now spent $65 million over the last fifteen years trying to save that particular kind of rat.

Now, we're not accusing the Key Largo wood rat of spreading hantavirus, mind you. We would never do that. This is America, after all, and a rat is presumed innocent until proved guilty.

A rat has a right
If it doesn't bite,
To pursue the lifestyle it's pursuing.
But it's perfectly clear
That our right hand, I fear,
Doesn't know what our left hand is doing.

Defense
Mergers

Although analysts worry that America's defense industry has become concentrated in too few hands, the Pentagon will spend a billion dollars or so this year helping weapons makers to merge. This is supposed to be saving the taxpayers money.

In 1993, there were twenty-one major defense aerospace contractors. Today there are five: Boeing, Raytheon, Litton Industries, Lockheed Martin and Northrop-Grumman. You can hear the consolidation in the names of some of them, as one company folded into another. This was done with the help and encouragement of the Pentagon, although earlier this year Defense Secretary William Cohen blocked yet another mega-merger between Northrop-Grumman and Lockheed Martin because of genuine concern about the rapidly shrinking list of companies to deal with and the consequent shrinking of competition.

The idea of all these mergers is to save money, with most of that savings going into lower prices for the planes and missiles. Most of the savings come from layoffs, by the way. The seven merged defense companies have cut eighteen thousand jobs. And the Pentagon encourages this by paying relocation costs, worker retraining, severance and plant closing expenses, amounting so far to about $800 million, sure to go over a billion by the end of the year. A drop in the bucket, admittedly, considering that the defense spending is $268 billion. So are the planes and missiles *really* costing less now? The contractors say, oh yes, they'd be higher if it weren't for the consolidation. But the General Accounting Office says that so many other factors affect the price of a weapon that they can't really tell.

One day there'll be one company when all the others are gone.
Boeing-Litton-Northrop-Grumman-Lockheed-Martin-
    Raytheon.
Called RaBoLitNorGrumLoktheon for short.
Or something of the sort.

Modernizing the
Modernization Program

In the government, as in the private sector, big organizations tend to be resistant to change. The more people there are in an organization, the more people are going to be throwing monkey wrenches into every effort to modernize or improve it. Of course, not every modernization is an improvement. But any proposed change is sure to be seen by some people as a threat.

For years now, a decade at least, the Internal Revenue Service has been trying to modernize its computer system. It reportedly spent $4 billion over the last ten years on the Tax System Modernization Project (TSMP), the goal of which has been to create an efficient and paperless system to process your tax return and mine and two hundred million others.

But have they done that? The answer, in a word, is no. But the IRS says that the good news is they have saved $1.5 billion to $2 billion by canceling twenty-six modernization projects. Deputy Treasury Secretary Lawrence Summers tells Congress that the IRS' ten-year modernization program was badly in need of modernization. Its complete overhaul of the agency's computer system needed a complete overhaul. Summers is the man overseeing the modernization of the IRS modernization and the overhauling of its overhaul. Yesterday the IRS brass appeared before a House appropriations subcommittee. This is the subcommittee that oversees the people who are overseeing the people who are modernizing the modernization program.

Mr. Summers was asked the following question: "Has there been an effort to identify those persons who have been at the root of a lot of the problems historically so that we can be sure the problem is not being perpetuated?" In other words, how do you know the same people who screwed up before aren't going to be screwing up again? Summers replied that such an analysis had been conducted but probably not in writing. Ah-ha. So they're doing it in their heads, I guess.

Summers doesn't want to point any fingers, obviously, but he says, "We did something rare in government. We announced the problem, we brought in new people, we're stopping funding things that were questionable." He's talking about the twenty-six IRS modernization overhauls the IRS has now killed as opposed to the ones they're now modernizing and overhauling.

This has been another in our series: Your Government at Work.

IX.

Inspiration

Mama Bair

Anna Bair shows up for work at the Fessler Knitting Company in Orwigsburg, Pennsylvania, at six o'clock sharp every morning. Her full-time job is stitching hems on sleeves and shirt bottoms. That's what she does all day. Some of the women take breaks, but not Anna Bair. She gets a certain rhythm going and likes to keep at it, working fast, sewing twenty-two dozen pieces an hour until her shift ends at three P.M.

Anna's been working there at Fessler since 1939. That's right—sixty years she's been there. Must have been a young girl when she started, you say? Well, no, she was forty. And she could have retired forty years ago, but she didn't want to and still doesn't. "You're never too old to work," she says. And she should know. Anna Bair is one hundred years old.

"She's always here," says her boss, Walter Meck. "The weather doesn't stop her. Illness doesn't stop her. Broken sewing machines don't stop her."

"I don't know what the big deal is," says Mrs. Bair. "There are lots of people around who are older than I am." Well, that may be true, but not very many of them are working full-time, the way she is. But she says she enjoys it. "I enjoy being with the girls," she says.

Her fellow employees love her. They threw a party for her a couple of weeks ago to celebrate her hundredth birthday.

But all work and no play wouldn't do, so every other Saturday, Anna and some of her younger friends, in their seventies and eighties, board a bus to Atlantic City, and they spend the day at the Tropicana Casino. Anna plays the slots.

One time, she hit a big payoff at the half dollar machine just before it was time to leave, and she didn't have time to exchange the coins. That time, she says, the bucket of coins was so heavy she could hardly lift it. The bus driver had to help her get back on the bus.

Mrs. Bair is a widow. From her two marriages, she has thirty-six children, grandchildren, great-grandchildren and great-great-grandchildren. At age one hundred, Anna Bair is not only alive, but alive and well. And working and playing and enjoying life. God bless you, Anna Bair.

Taps

A seventy-year-old man by the name of John Bradley died of a stroke recently at Langlade Memorial Hospital in Antigo, Wisconsin. Maybe you didn't know his name, but you knew him. You have seen him countless times. The image of John Bradley and the others pushing, straining, reaching, striving is burned into the American soul.

The date was February 23, 1945. Bradley, a boatswain's mate second class in the U.S. Navy, saw some Marines trying to raise the American flag on a rocky hill called Mount Suribachi on a bloody island called Iwo Jima, and he went to help them.

Joe Rosenthal, an Associated Press photographer, won the Pulitzer Prize for the picture he took a few moments later. Earlier that day, four days after the U.S. Marines invaded Iwo

Jima, another flag, a smaller one, had been raised there. That was the first time in World War II that the American flag had been raised over Japanese territory.

The commanding officer thought that flag was too little. He wanted a big flag up there, a great big one, so that the Americans down below—and the Japanese too—could see Old Glory flying from that mountaintop.

But this time the flag was so big and there was so much wind up there that it was hard to handle. The five U.S. Marines were struggling, and so the U.S. Navy, in the person of John Bradley, jumped in to help. And at the perfect instant, Joe Rosenthal snapped his camera shutter and froze in time a picture so classic and so glorious that it looked like a statue.

Indeed, it is a statue now, too. The U.S. Marine Iwo Jima Memorial near Arlington National Cemetery is modeled after Joe Rosenthal's photograph.

(A bugle plays "Taps.")

John Bradley was the last of the six men in that tableau. Ira Hayes, a Native American from Arizona, died in 1955. René Gagnon, of Manchester, New Hampshire, died in 1979. The three others were killed in the fighting, along with 6,818 other Americans and 21,000 Japanese in the battle of Iwo Jima. John Bradley was seventy when he died. The "Taps" was for him, and for all those others.

Doing the
Right Thing

At a time when some people are pinching pennies, there are still some big spenders around. And at a time when cheating abounds and some say ethics and values have all but disappeared in this country, there are still honest people around. "I'm one of them," says Ken Allen of Saint Petersburg, Florida.

Ken is twenty-one years old, and he works on the valet parking team at a hotel there. The other day he had what must have seemed a valet's dream. He got a customer's Cadillac from the garage, brought it around front. The man handed him a tip, got in the car and drove off. Ken looked down at the bills in his hand, and the first one was a hundred-dollar bill. And he peeled it back and looked at the next one. That was a hundred, too. And so was the next one and the next one, and the one after that. There were ten of them altogether. It was a thousand-dollar tip. Wow! What a break!

But the more Ken thought about it, the more it seemed it was too good to be true. And a little inner voice told him, "This is a mistake." And indeed it was.

As elated as Ken Allen felt when he looked down and realized how much money the customer had given him as a tip, that is how dejected Harold Birthy felt when he looked down and realized how much money he had handed to the guy who had brought the car around. "I'm poor folk," says Birthy. "I've grown up scrapping for nickels and dimes."

By the time he realized what he'd done, Birthy was well on his way up the road to West Virginia. It wasn't until he reached in his pocket to pay for some gas at a gas station that he missed the money and started to panic. "You can't imagine how I felt," he said.

Though he figured what was gone was gone, he thought it might be worth a try anyway to get it back. So he put in a call to the hotel, and to his amazement, the manager told him, "Oh, we have your money right here, sir. The young man turned it all in."

As lovely as it had been to get a thousand-dollar tip, young Ken Allen figured, well, he may be lucky, but he wasn't that lucky. So he had taken the $1,000 to his boss, just in case the customer called.

Well, Ken ended up with a tip, all right, $20. Is he resentful at getting only twenty of Harold Birthy's $1,000? "Not at all," says Ken. "You have got to feel good that he got his thousand dollars back. There are still honest people," he says, "and I'm one of them."

Not a big story. It won't make headlines or the tabloids, but I love hearing about that. Don't you?

Big Mama's
Birthday

atonya Baldwin organized a birthday party over the weekend for Luree Peterson of Century, Florida, known to the family as Big Mama. Big Mama had told family members she was afraid they'd forget her birthday. Not likely, considering that this was Luree Peterson's 110th birthday. Big Mama is Latonya Baldwin's great-great-great-grandma. Latonya is one of her six great-great-great-grandchildren.

When Luree Peterson and her husband moved into the house he'd built for them in Century, Florida, it was 1940. He'd just started working at the Alger Sullivan Lumber Company. The name Century didn't mean anything special to her then. It was only ten years ago, when she celebrated her hundredth birthday in Century, that she realized *she* was at the century mark.

Century was where she had raised so many kids and grandkids and great-grandkids. Now, ten years later, two of her five children are still alive, and nineteen of her grandchildren. And ninety-six great-grandchildren. And 124 great-great-grandchildren. And six great-great-great-grandchildren, including Latonya. That's 241 people altogether—and no way they were going to forget.

At the birthday party, one of her granddaughters, Josephine Hayes, gave Big Mama a teddy bear that sings "Wild thing . . . I think I love you." That's a song that had not been written when Luree was born, in 1889. Now, as to Big Mama's secret of longevity: If you want to live a long time, says Luree Peterson, never let yourself get tired. She says long life is the result of clean living, good genes, faith and a good night's sleep every night.

"I worked night and day," she says, "and when I went to sleep, I went to sleep."

And she says this is why she is still pretty spry,
Although not quite as spry as back when.
But she says don't feel bad, you may slow down a tad
When you are a hundred and ten.

Alvin Saltzman's
Purple Heart

Over the weekend, Alvin Saltzman got his Purple Heart. It had been a long time coming. Mr. Saltzman is sixty-six years old now, and the military action in which he was wounded took place at 6:45 A.M. on the fourth of December in the year 1950.

It was the Korean War. U.S. Marine Private Alvin Saltzman was twenty years old. His unit was pulling back from the Yalu River to the Chosin Reservoir when it came under an intensive mortar barrage from the North Koreans. Everybody in Saltzman's squad was killed, or so it was thought. The bodies were zipped into body bags.

It was not until a medic by the name of J. P. Greene saw one of those body bags move that they realized the young Marine was still alive. Just barely, but still breathing, his heart still beating. Greene then carried Saltzman two miles to safety.

Three weeks later, Saltzman was lying in a hospital with wounds over 70 percent of his body when General Douglas MacArthur himself visited and passed out Purple Hearts to the wounded men. But somehow, he accidentally passed by Saltzman's bed and didn't realize there was anyone in it. And although he had earned one, Saltzman received no Purple Heart that day, or afterwards. And in time, the paperwork was lost. As it happens, his particular unit had burned a lot of its paperwork to prevent it from falling into enemy hands. There was no official proof of what had happened.

Then a few months ago, Saltzman petitioned the Marine Corps and included letters from other Korean War vets verifying that the story was true; that he had, indeed, been wounded in Korea. One of the letters was from J. P. Greene, the medic who had seen the body bag move and who had carried him out of harm's way. There was an investigation. The red tape was cleared away.

And on Saturday, Alvin Saltzman, now sixty-six, stood tall before Marine Lieutenant Colonel Mark Breun and accepted the Purple Heart with a salute. You could see as he walked away that Mr. Saltzman walks with a slight limp, another souvenir of that morning in 1950. Now, at least, at last, he has the Purple Heart to go with it.

Will Wonders
Never Cease

It's always interesting to go through your old high school year-
book. You don't look the same in that picture, do you?
Anybody you still know has changed a lot, too. And, of course,
those you've lost track of—who knows what became of them
or what they look like now? You might not even recognize
them. And where are they now? Where's the one who was vale-
dictorian, class president, the most popular, the best student?
You wonder whatever happened. Did the most likely to succeed succeed? And how about those least likely to succeed? Did
they fail or have they fooled everybody and done well—all
those who struggled and just barely made it: the C students?
And not being scholars, they weren't the ones who would get
the college scholarships, either.

Ed Cease knew all about that, but he was one of those who fooled everybody. He went on to make millions in real estate. But he never forgot. And this week, something amazing:

Broward Community College in Fort Lauderdale, Florida, just got the biggest bequest in its history. Edward Cease, a multimillionaire who died in March at the age of eighty-six, left the college a third of his estate—$4.5 million—to be used, he said, for scholarships for C students. He figured the A students and the B students would do all right. But he remembered from his own youth that, as he said in his will, "C students are often capable of greater accomplishment when relieved of the problems of outside employment while attending school."

He wanted his money to go to, in his words, "industrious persons who would show promise, preferably from Broward schools," and if there weren't enough C students to take advantage of these scholarships, why, then, Mr. Cease said, "the money could be awarded to students who got higher grades."

Tuition is only about $2,000 a year at Broward Community College. And so the proceeds of Ed Cease's bequest are going to benefit some 250 new students a year. Cease did not go to Broward. The college is thirty-five years old. He went to school longer ago than that, but he never forgot. And this week it became clear that he remembered in spectacular fashion.

A one-of-a-kind story, you say? Then look at this:

Lansing Porter Moore was a Dartmouth man, class of 1937, president of the Dartmouth Club of Long Island, generous donor and fund-raiser for Dartmouth's capital campaigns and annual funds, active in Dartmouth alumni activities for fifty years, including reunions and class trips.

When he died in 1990 at the age of seventy-five, his wife, Florence, gave Dartmouth $2 million in his memory. There is now a Lansing Porter Moore Theater at Dartmouth's Hopkins Center. And just recently it was announced that Mrs. Moore, when she died, left another $18.2 million to the college, the largest bequest in Dartmouth's history.

In preparing the information in connection with this remarkable bequest, Dartmouth did some research and discovered that Lansing Porter Moore did not graduate with the rest of his class in 1937. In checking the records, they were astonished by what else they found, or should I say didn't find.

When Dartmouth discovered that Lansing Porter Moore was not given a diploma at commencement ceremonies in 1937, they checked to see if he got his degree some year after that or some year before. But there is no record of a Lansing Porter Moore ever graduating from Dartmouth. In fact, no one by that name was enrolled at Dartmouth in 1937 or the year before that or the year before that.

Here was a man for whom the Moore Theater had been named. Here was a man whose love for Dartmouth was such that Dartmouth is now $20 million richer with the gift made in his memory. But the only record of his having attended Dartmouth at all was for three months in 1933, his freshman year, after which, apparently, he dropped out. Nineteen thirty-three was the bottom of the Great Depression; a lot of college students had to drop out back then.

Dartmouth officials knew Moore from his alumni activities, but never realized he'd only been there as a student for three short months and left and never came back as a student. They don't know whether Mrs. Moore was aware of that, either, or whether he'd ever mentioned it to her in the twenty-six years they were married.

Dartmouth plans to use the Moore bequest for two scholarships named for Moore's sons and to name the new psychology building after the Moore family. Twenty million dollars to Dartmouth, where he'd been a student for only twelve weeks back in 1933. It must have been some twelve weeks. He may have been a Dartmouth student for only three months, but ever after, Lansing Porter Moore was a Dartmouth man.

The Fake Who Was
the Real Thing

This is the story of a Vietnam War veteran who was a hero, earned himself a chest full of medals and a promotion to sergeant, even though he had never really been a private, never enlisted, wasn't drafted and was told officially that he was physically unfit to serve.

Nobody would ever have known that Paul Maher was a fake if he hadn't decided six years ago that he was proud of what he did and he wanted recognition for it. So he asked his congressman for help in getting that recognition.

Last week, the Army's Board for Correction of Military Records announced that it was creating a file. It usually corrects files, but this time it created one to show that Maher served in Vietnam, saved the life of at least one other soldier and was honorably discharged.

What happened was that in 1966, at the age of nineteen, Maher was exempted from military service because of a steel pin in his arm, put there when he fractured his arm wrestling with another kid when he was thirteen. The other kid was Frank Klaus, Jr. At the time, Klaus was drafted, but he went AWOL, and he and Maher cooked up a little plot to get Klaus out of the Army. Maher would show up at Fort Dix and say he was Klaus and that there had been a mistake and that he should get a medical discharge.

What happened was that when Maher showed up there, they put him in the barracks with AWOL soldiers and shipped them to Vietnam. He didn't know how to be a soldier, but he imitated people around him, and after two months, he was able to fake it pretty well.

In Vietnam, he served with the Second Battalion, 27th Infantry Regiment of the 25th Infantry Division near Pu Chi. He fought in combat missions, saved one of his buddies from drowning, won numerous medals and citations.

Well, the Record Correction Board, after examining dental records, fingerprints and handwriting, ruled that while the board does not approve of the deceptive manner in which he initiated his service, it cannot be denied he served and that he served well. In fact, the Board went on, considering his lack of formal preparation, his performance as an infantryman in combat was extraordinary.

It's still not clear whether both Klaus and Maher might be subject to prosecution for the switch they made or whether Maher is eligible for veteran's benefits. As for Maher, he wasn't the real thing, but he turned out to be the real thing.

Secrets of
Longevity

In Orlando, at the Miranda Nursing and Rehabilitation
Center, an old woman named Mary Thompson has died of a
heart attack. We all die of something sooner or later, but Mary
Thompson died way later in life than most people. Nobody
knows for sure how old she was. She never did get a birth cer-
tificate. But the Social Security Administration has records on
her dating back to March 27, 1876, which would mean that
Mary Thompson was at least 120 years old. She was surely the
oldest person in the United States and may even have been
older than Jeanne Calment, the Frenchwoman who turned 121
in February. And if so, Mary Thompson would have been the
oldest person in the world.

What was it about this daughter of slaves that made her live so long? Scientists don't know what causes human aging or what chemical systems are involved, although a major theory is that substances called free radicals have something to do with it. And they're just now isolating the gene that makes tiny soil-dwelling, bacteria-eating worms called sea eligans live longer when the so-called "aged-one" gene is mutated. Whether there's some related gene that controls how long we humans live, we can't say for sure. Maybe longevity runs in your family. If your parents live to a ripe old age, there's a good chance you will, too.

As for Mary Thompson, the woman who died in Orlando recently, she outlived two husbands and eight of her ten children. At the Miranda Center where she lived, they say she was easygoing, always had a nice little smile, never seemed to get angry, or if she did, she didn't stay angry long. All her life, she never smoked or drank alcohol. She worked regularly in the yard until she was 105. Mary Thompson was a baby when Alexander Graham Bell invented the telephone. She was at least twenty-seven when the Wright Brothers flew at Kitty Hawk. She was at least sixty-five when the Japanese attacked Pearl Harbor. When the country celebrated its 200th birthday, she was at least a hundred. They say she enjoyed chocolate candy and music and watching television. Television didn't come along, of course, until she was over seventy.

Whenever Mary Thompson was asked the secret to her longevity, she would give the following good advice: "Live a clean life and mind your own business." Makes sense to me.